CAMPAIGN 411

THE KAMENETS-PODOLSKY POCKET 1944

Encirclement of Hube's 1st Panzer Army

ROBERT FORCZYK   ILLUSTRATED BY ADAM HOOK

OSPREY PUBLISHING
Bloomsbury Publishing Plc
Kemp House, Chawley Park, Cumnor Hill, Oxford OX2 9PH, UK
29 Earlsfort Terrace, Dublin 2, Ireland
1385 Broadway, 5th Floor, New York, NY 10018, USA
E-mail: info@ospreypublishing.com
www.ospreypublishing.com

OSPREY is a trademark of Osprey Publishing Ltd

First published in Great Britain in 2025

© Osprey Publishing Ltd, 2025

A catalogue record for this book is available from the British Library.

ISBN: PB 9781472862266; eBook 9781472862273; ePDF 9781472862280; XML 9781472862259

25 26 27 28 29   10 9 8 7 6 5 4 3 2 1

Maps by Bounford.com
3D BEVs by Paul Kime
Index by Mark Swift
Typeset by PDQ Digital Media Solutions, Bungay, UK
Printed by Repro India Ltd.

MIX
Paper
FSC   FSC® C047271

Osprey Publishing supports the Woodland Trust, the UK's leading woodland conservation charity.

To find out more about our authors and books visit
www.ospreypublishing.com. Here you will find extracts, author interviews, details of forthcoming events and the option to sign up for our newsletter.

Note on place names

Most of the populated places in this region had either Polish or Russian names until after World War II. During the war, the Germans often referred to locations by their Polish nomenclature. Some towns/villages in Galicia also had Yiddish names. In the past several decades, Ukraine has imposed its nomenclature on the towns in this region, sometimes substituting entirely new names. In this work, I will typically use nomenclature as it appeared on 1944 maps and documentation.

Glossary

AOK	Armee Oberkommando (Army-level formation)
APBC	armour-piercing ballistic capped (ammunition)
APCR	armour-piercing composite rigid (ammunition)
BAD	Bombardirovochnaya Aviatsionnaya Diviziya (Bomber Aviation Division)
BAK	Bombardirovochnaya Aviatsionnyi Korpus (Bomber Aviation Corps)
FEB	Feldersatz-Bataillon (Field Replacement Battalion)
GA	Gvardeyskaya Armiya (Guard Army)
GKO	Gosudarstvennyï komitet oborony (State Defence Committee)
GRC	Guards Rifle Corps
GRD	Guards Rifle Division
GTA	Gvardeyskaya Tankovaya Armiya (Guards Tank Army)
GTB	Guards Tank Brigade
GTC	Gvardeyskiye tankovyye korpusa (Guards Tank Corps)
HKL	*Hauptkampflinie* (main line of resistance)
IAD	Isrebitel'naya Aviatsionnyi Diviziya (Fighter Aviation Division)
IAK	Isrebitel'naya Aviatsionnyi Korpus (Fighter Aviation Corps)
JG	Jagdgeschwader (Fighter Group)
KG	Kampfgeschwader (Bomber Group)
LSSAH	1. SS-Panzer-Division *Leibstandarte SS Adolf Hitler*
NKO	Narodny Komissariat Oborony (People's Commissariat of Defence)
OKH	Oberkommando des Heeres (Army High Command)
PzAOK	Panzerarmee Oberkommando (Panzer Army)
PzKpfw	Panzerkampfwagen (AFV, armoured fighting vehicle)
RVGK	Rezerv Verhovnogo Glavnokomandovanija (Stavka Reserve)
ShAD	Shturovoy Aviatsionnyi Diviziya (Ground Attack Aviation Division)
ShAK	Shturovoy Aviatsionnyi Korpus (Ground Attack Aviation Corps)
s.Pz.Abt	schwere Panzer-Abteilung (Heavy Tank Battalion)
SPW	Schützenpanzerwagen (armoured infantry vehicle)
StuG	Sturmgeschütz (assault gun)
TA	Tankovyye armii (Tank Army)
VA	Vozdushnaya Armiya (Air Army)
VVS	Voyenno-Vozdushnye Sily (Soviet Air Force)

Key to military symbols

XXXXX Army Group	XXXX Army	XXX Corps
XX Division	X Brigade	III Regiment
II Battalion	I Company/Battery	••• Platoon
•• Section	• Squad	Infantry
Artillery	Cavalry	Airborne
Unit HQ	Air defence	Air Force
Air mobile	Air transportable	Amphibious
Anti-tank	Armour	Air aviation
Bridging	Engineer	Headquarters
Maintenance	Medical	Missile
Mountain	Navy	Nuclear, biological, chemical
Ordnance	Parachute	Reconnaissance
Signal	Supply	Transport movement
Rocket artillery	Air defence artillery	

Key to unit identification

Unit Identifier — Parent unit
Commander
(+) with added elements
(−) less elements

Front cover main illustration: The crossing of the Zbruch River at Skala-Podilska, 31 March 1944. (Adam Hook)
Title page photograph: A Soviet SU-76 self-propelled gun passes an abandoned German 8.8cm Flak gun in Chernovtsy. (Author)

CONTENTS

ORIGINS OF THE CAMPAIGN

After the failure of the German summer offensive at Kursk in July 1943, the Soviet Red Army began a series of multi-front counteroffensives which rapidly pushed Generalfeldmarschall Erich von Manstein's Heeresgruppe Süd (Army Group South) back across Ukraine toward the Dnepr River. Hitler and the OKH quickly drafted a plan to create a defensive line behind the Dnepr, known as the Panther–Wotan Stellung, to provide von Manstein's hard-pressed forces with a secure position in which to reorganize. However, General Nikolai Vatutin's Voronezh Front was able to seize a bridgehead over the Dnepr River at Bukrin on 22 September 1943. Three days later, General-polkovnik Ivan Konev's Steppe Front also seized a bridgehead across the Dnepr, farther south near Kremenchug. Once closed up on the Dnepr, Vatutin's Voronezh Front was re-designated as the 1st Ukrainian Front and Konev's Steppe Front was re-designated as the 2nd Ukrainian Front. Although von Manstein's forces fought furiously to contain the Soviet bridgeheads, the Red Army gradually increased its foothold and managed to conduct a surprise attack that captured Kiev on 6 November. In response, Hitler agreed to transfer strong armoured reinforcements from the West to reinforce von Manstein's command, but the subsequent German counterattacks in November–December 1943 failed to reverse the deteriorating situation.

No sooner had von Manstein's counteroffensive culminated, than Vatutin mounted his own very powerful offensive on 24 December. Vatutin attacked Generaloberst Erhard Raus' 4. Panzerarmee with seven armies and quickly overwhelmed the thinly held German front line. Within a week, General-polkovnik Pavel S. Rybalko's 3rd Guards Tank Army (3GTA) had taken Zhitomir and von Manstein's left flank was nearly broken. Rybalko's 3GTA then pivoted southward and began advancing toward Vinnitsa. Von Manstein requested authorization to transfer part of Generaloberst Hans-Valentin Hube's 1. Panzerarmee westward to support Generaloberst Erhard Raus' 4. Panzerarmee's crumbling front, but Hitler forbade this movement. Nevertheless, von Manstein decided to deceive Hitler, and on 1 January 1944 began quietly transferring General der Panzertruppen Hermann Breith's III Panzerkorps to Uman. While von Manstein's unauthorized transfer did help to slow Vatutin's advance, the transfer of Hube's army weakened the German forces opposing Konev's 2nd Ukrainian Front. As soon as Konev recognized that Hube's 1. Panzerarmee had shifted laterally to the west, he launched his own offensive on 5 January against the German 8. Armee. Three days later, the 5th Guards Tank Army captured Kirovograd and pushed the 8. Armee back on its heels.

With both his left and right flanks now bending under heavy pressure, von Manstein's real problem was the boundary between the 1. Panzerarmee and the 8. Armee, near Korsun. The Germans still held a small section of frontage along the Dnepr River in the Korsun–Cherkassy sector and Hitler was adamant that it was not to be abandoned. Yet the advances by Vatutin and Konev had turned the Korsun sector into a salient with very vulnerable flanks. Von Manstein wanted to evacuate the salient and form a shorter, more defensible line, but Hitler refused and became very irritated with constant requests for withdrawals. Unable to evacuate the Korsun salient, von Manstein decided to scrape together his best remaining mobile forces to create an armoured reserve to deal with the inevitable Soviet offensive. Breith's III Panzerkorps was designated as the primary component, reinforced with an ad hoc tank group known as schwere-Panzer-Regiment 'Bäke' (a mixed Kampfgruppe of Panther and Tiger tanks). Yet Vatutin kept the pressure on Raus' battered 4. Panzerarmee, pushing steadily toward Vinnitsa and the German supply base at Uman with General-leytenant Mikhail Katukov's 1st Tank Army (1TA). Consequently, von Manstein was forced to prematurely commit Breith's III Panzerkorps in Operation *Watutin* on 24 January, in order to stop Katukov's 1TA from reaching Uman. While the counterattack succeeded in encircling some Soviet units and halting the 1TA, it also committed virtually all of von Manstein's mobile reserves to this one sector.

In Moscow, Marshal Georgi K. Zhukov also recognized the vulnerability of the Korsun salient, and he ordered Vatutin and Konev to mount a coordinated pincer attack to isolate and destroy the German forces in this sector. On 25 January 1944, Konev's 2nd Ukrainian Front struck the east side of the Korsun salient with General-polkovnik Pavel A. Rotmistrov's 5th Guards Tank Army (5GTA), and the next day, Vatutin's 1st Ukrainian Front attacked the west side of the salient with General-leytenant Andrei G. Kravchenko's 6th Tank Army (6TA). German tactical reserves were able to delay, but not stop the Soviet armoured pincers. Consequently, by 28 January the converging Soviet spearheads were able to link up, completing the encirclement of six divisions with nearly 59,000 German troops in the Korsun Pocket. Von Manstein was determined not to repeat the mistakes made with the encircled 6. Armee at Stalingrad one year prior and he moved quickly to mount a rescue mission to save the troops in the Korsun Pocket. He began by terminating Operation *Watutin* in order to shift Breith's III Panzerkorps east to attack into the flank of General-leytenant Kravchenko's 6TA. Von Manstein also ordered the 8. Armee to commit its XXXXVII Panzerkorps against the flank of Rotmistrov's 5GTA. Von Manstein's relief operation was designated Operation *Wanda* and he hoped that prompt action would enable his understrength Panzer units to punch through to the Korsun Pocket before the Soviets could crush the encircled forces. Inside the pocket,

German infantry man a thin trench line in open steppe, early 1944. The lack of adequate numbers of well-trained and equipped infantry or suitable terrain obstacles to impede Soviet armoured advances prevented Heeresgruppe Süd from creating a viable defensive line in the western Ukraine. (Author)

Von Manstein committed virtually all of his available armour to the Korsun Pocket relief operation in February 1944. Although partly successful, the effort left most of 1. Panzerarmee's tank units exhausted and in poor condition to resist Zhukov's next round of offensives. (Author)

the 5. SS-Panzer-Division *Wiking* and five infantry divisions merged into Gruppe Stemmermann, which contracted in order to create a defensible perimeter around the small airfield near Korsun.

Operating primarily from airfields around Uman, the Luftwaffe was tasked with flying in enough supplies – roughly 70 tons per day – to keep Stemmermann's troops combat-capable until the relief operation could reach them. Beginning on 31 January, three Gruppen of Ju 52 transports were able to fly in 2,026 tons of supplies during the 17-day airlift operation and fly out about 2,400 wounded troops. Unlike Stalingrad, the German soldiers in the Korsun Pocket were not starving, but morale was tenuous and troops could become apathetic if not constantly engaged in productive tasks. Although the distance between Uman and Korsun was only 106km, the Luftwaffe suffered heavy losses from enemy opposition and adverse weather conditions. Altogether, 32 Ju 52 transports were lost during the Kuban airlift operation and many of the remainder were damaged. It is important to note that the Luftwaffe was simultaneously conducting a large-scale airlift to support the isolated Axis garrison in the Crimea – further stretching German theatre logistic capabilities.

General der Panzertruppen Nikolaus von Vormann's XXXXVII Panzerkorps attacked with two divisions (the 11. and 13. Panzer-Divisionen) on 1 February and initially made good progress through Konev's outer screening forces. However, von Vormann's Panzers were soon stopped at the Shpolka River when a bridge collapsed. German engineers managed to erect a pontoon bridge, but half of von Vormann's tanks were PzKpfw V Panthers, which were too heavy to cross. Meanwhile, Breith's III Panzerkorps struggled to reach its assembly areas due to the thick Ukrainian mud and thus, could not join the relief operation until 4 February. Breith's corps was fairly strong, with a total of 126 operational tanks and assault guns in the 16. and 17. Panzer-Divisionen and schwere-Panzer-Regiment 'Bäke', and von Manstein promised two more Panzer-Divisionen as reinforcements. As with von Vormann, Breith's corps was able to advance 19km on the first day of its attack, but became stalled at the Gniloi Tikich River due to mud, inadequate engineering support and limited fuel supplies. Vatutin quickly shifted Kravchenko's 6th Tank Army into Breith's path, halting the German advance 36km short of the link-up with Gruppe Stemmermann.

Once the relief columns had been halted, Vatutin and Konev focused on reducing the pocket, but they decided to rely primarily upon artillery in order to conserve their limited amount of front-line infantry. Von Manstein reinforced Breith's depleted III Panzerkorps with the 1. Panzer-Division and a Kampfgruppe from the 1. SS-Panzer-Division *Leibstandarte SS Adolf Hitler* (*LSSAH*), increasing its armoured strength to 155 tanks and assault guns (including 80 Panthers). On the morning of 11 February, Breith resumed his attack, with Bäke's heavy tank in the lead. One Kampfgruppe succeeded in crossing the Gniloi Tikich River at Frankovka while another captured the town of Lisyanka. Von Vormann's XXXXVII Panzerkorps also attacked and made some progress toward a link-up, before running out of steam. For a brief moment on 13 February, it seemed that von Manstein's forces would relieve the Korsun Pocket. However, the dire shortage of fuel in the forward units immobilized the German tanks.

Although caught off balance by the sudden display of German tactical agility, the Soviet commanders recovered and made countermoves. Zhukov provided Vatutin with four tank brigades from the 2nd Tank Army in the Stavka Reserve (RVGK), which were sent to block Breith's Panzers. Refuelled by airdrop, Breith made one more short sprint on 13 February, before being stopped 10km short of reaching Gruppe Stemmermann. Von Manstein's relief operation could go no farther. On the same day, Konev's forces overran the Korsun airfield, terminating the airlift to Gruppe Stemmermann. The Stavka also committed several regiments of the new IS-1 heavy tanks, equipped with the D-5T 85mm gun, to oppose Breith's dwindling number of Panthers and Tigers.

Recognizing that the forces within the pocket would not remain combat-capable much longer, von Manstein ordered Stemmermann to begin attacking toward Breith's III Panzerkorps. On the night of 16/17 February, Gruppe Stemmermann began its breakout attack. Although the German infantry were able to infiltrate partly through the Soviet perimeter, they were eventually detected and the result was a wild stampede by over 50,000 German troops. Stemmermann was killed and the breakout became a disaster when troops encountered the unfrozen 30m-wide Gniloi Tikich River. Eventually, over 35,000 German troops managed to reach Breith's III Panzerkorps at Lisyanka, but they had lost virtually all of their equipment (including 50 tanks and assault guns plus over 300 artillery pieces) in escaping from the Korsun Pocket. Not only were six German divisions removed from von Manstein's order of battle, but many of the survivors were physically unfit to resume front-line service and had to be sent to the rear to recover. It would take six months just to rebuild the elite SS-Panzer-Division *Wiking*. Thus, while Vatutin and Konev were chagrined by the German escape, they still had succeeded in eliminating two corps, which von Manstein could not replace. Stalin and Konev papered over the German breakout and falsely claimed that almost all of the German troops in the Korsun Pocket were captured or killed.

Hube's 1. Panzerarmee suffered about 4,000 casualties during Operation *Wanda* and lost 156 tanks (most due to mechanical failure). By the end of the Korsun fighting, Breith's III Panzerkorps was reduced to just 60 operational tanks and six assault guns. Hube's best troops were left exhausted by weeks of extended winter combat, with no hope of relief in sight. Ironically, von Manstein

German equipment abandoned in the Korsun Pocket, including a PzKpfw IV tank from the SS-Panzer-Division *Wiking*. Even a fairly successful breakout occupation still resulted in a huge loss of materiel, which left surviving units nearly disarmed. (Courtesy of the Central Museum of the Armed Forces, Moscow via Stavka)

had managed to save the lives of two-thirds of the troops in the Korsun Pocket, but at the cost of seriously depleting his armoured reserves. By early March 1944, von Manstein's Heeresgruppe Süd had suffered over 141,000 combat casualties in the previous three months (including 50,000 dead or missing), but received only 132,000 replacements. When non-combat losses are factored in, Heeresgruppe Süd had been reduced by over 100,000 men in just three months. German losses in equipment on the Eastern Front in this period had also been massive, with nearly 1,400 tanks lost (including 351 Panthers and 140 Tigers) – equivalent to 70 per cent of total tank production. Rather surprisingly, only half of German monthly tank production was going to the Eastern Front, with the rest going to build up armoured reserves in Western Europe and the Italian front. Under these conditions, it was unlikely that von Manstein would be able to replenish his armoured reserve before the Soviets mounted another major offensive in the western Ukraine.

Nor was Zhukov inclined to give von Manstein any kind of respite, and he pushed for the Stavka to quickly begin planning the next round of offensives even before the fighting around Korsun had concluded. Soviet losses in the Battle of the Korsun Pocket had been heavy, with Vatutin's 1st Ukrainian Front suffering about 50,000 casualties and losing 500 tanks, while Konev's 2nd Ukrainian Front suffered about half as many losses. Nevertheless, the Stavka was in a far better position to replace its losses than the overextended Wehrmacht. Zhukov managed to secure the release of General-leytenant Vasily M. Badanov's 4th Tank Army (4TA) from the RVGK and assigned it to the 1st Ukrainian Front, as well as ensuring replacements to bring other depleted units up to strength. The most painful Soviet loss actually occurred after the end of the Korsun Pocket operation, when Vatutin was shot and mortally wounded by Ukrainian partisans on 28 February. Zhukov immediately stepped in and took command of the 1st Ukrainian Front, in place of Vatutin.

Despite the temporary halt of the Soviet offensive, Hube's 1. Panzerarmee was unable to rest and refit after the Battle of the Korsun Pocket. First,

German prisoners taken during the Battle of the Korsun Pocket, February 1944. About two-thirds of the encircled German troops managed to break out of the pocket and reach von Manstein's relief force, but over 10,000 troops were killed or captured in the attempt. Furthermore, none of the divisions that escaped was combat-capable after the breakout, which later influenced how von Manstein viewed the breakout of Hube's 1. Panzerarmee. (Author)

Breith's III Panzerkorps had to conduct a fighting withdrawal from the Lisyanka sector and help establish a new front line north of Uman, in conjunction with the 8. Armee. Second, Hube had to mend his weakened connections with Raus' 4. Panzerarmee on his left flank, which would require shifting some Panzer units up to 250km westward. The intractable dilemma facing von Manstein's Heeresgruppe Süd in March 1944 was that there were no natural lines of defence in the remaining portion of Axis-held western Ukraine, and Germany lacked the manpower, resources and time needed to create a viable front line. Under these conditions, retreat to shorter, more defensible lines was the only credible military strategy, but Hitler rejected this line of thinking as defeatist.

Looking at the thinly held enemy front line after the Battle of Korsun, Zhukov could see that von Manstein's left flank was extremely weak, because Raus' 4. Panzerarmee was holding a 240km-wide front with barely a dozen badly depleted divisions (including SS-Polizei and security units). While virtually all of von Manstein's Panzers had been focused on the Korsun situation, Vatutin had taken advantage of the enemy's distraction by sending his 13th and 60th Armies to attack the left wing of Raus' 4. Panzerarmee. Raus did not have a continuous front in the Rovno–Lutsk sector and the decimated XIII Armeekorps was unable to prevent the 60th Army from seizing both cities by 11 February, which put Vatutin's right flank across the pre-1939 border of Poland. Von Manstein hastily transferred the 7. and 8. Panzer-Divisionen to the Lutsk sector, which managed to prevent the collapse of Raus' left flank but weakened the centre of the 4. Panzerarmee sector around Tarnopol. The depleted German Panzer units were constantly being shifted to deal with local crises, but this only exposed the sectors they were drawn from, which invited new attacks. Zhukov, who was always looking for another massive encirclement operation like Stalingrad, saw Hube's 1. Panzerarmee as his next target. If Hube's army could be isolated and destroyed, or even just pushed back into northern Romania, the entire German front in south-west Ukraine would collapse. Thus, the Soviet victory in the Battle of the Korsun Pocket set the stage for an even more dramatic and large-scale battle of annihilation. The forthcoming campaign would bear several names, including the Battle of the Kamenets-Podolsky Pocket, the Proskurov–Chernovtsy offensive, or more popularly, Hube's Pocket.

The small city on the Smotrych River (a tributary of the Dniester River) that bore the name of this campaign has had many, many names, but Kamenets-Podolsky will serve as well as any of them. By the start of World War II, Kamenets-Podolsky had been in existence for nine centuries, and it had been intimately involved in the military history of the region stretching back to the Medieval period. Poles, Turks, Russians and Ukrainians had spilled significant amounts of blood trying to add this city to their domains, since it offered a useful border fortress. Hitler's invasion of the Soviet Union also stamped its indelible mark on the city, which was the site of the massacre of 23,600 Jews by SS-Polizei units in August 1941. By the time that the Red steamroller appeared on the horizon in March 1944, much of the population was gone and Kamenets-Podolsky was serving as a minor Wehrmacht logistics base. While certainly not as well known among English-speaking audiences as other Eastern Front campaigns, such as Kursk, Moscow or Stalingrad, the fighting around Kamenets-Podolsky in March–April 1944 would prove no less dramatic or consequential.

CHRONOLOGY

1944

24–30 January	1. Panzerarmee conducts Operation *Watutin*, a spoiling attack against the Soviet 1st Tank Army.
25–26 January	The Soviet 1st and 2nd Ukrainian Fronts begin their offensives against both sides of the Korsun salient.
28 January	Soviet armoured pincers close around two German corps in the Korsun Pocket.
1 February	Operation *Wanda*, the relief operation, begins.
16/17 February	Gruppe Stemmermann breaks out of Korsun Pocket.
18 February	The Stavka issues guidance for the next offensive to the 1st and 2nd Ukrainian Fronts (Stavka VGK Directive No. 22029).
23 February	Vatutin presents his operational plan for the offensive to the Stavka.
25 February	The Stavka approves Vatutin's plan.
28 February	Vatutin is badly wounded by Ukrainian partisans.
4 March	1st Ukrainian Front launches the first phase of its offensive in the Yampil–Shepetovka sector.
5 March	2nd Ukrainian Front attacks the boundary between the 1. Panzerarmee and 8. Armee.
6 March	3rd Guards Tank Army severs the main German rail line at Volochisk.
8 March	Hitler issues Führerbefehl No. 11, designating Tarnopol and Proskurov[1] as fortresses.
9 March	1st Guards Army captures Staro-Konstantinov.
10 March	Uman airfield is captured.
	An attempt by 60th Army to seize Tarnopol is repulsed.
11–12 March	4. Panzerarmee launches a counterattack in the Volochisk sector.
17 March	2nd Ukrainian Front (2TA) reaches Yampol on the Dniester River.
18 March	The 38th Army captures Zhmerynka.
19 March	2nd Ukrainian Front (6TA) reaches Mogilev-Podolsky.
	Operation *Margarethe* – the German occupation of Hungary.

---

1   Proskurov was renamed Khmelnytskyi after World War II.

20 March	The 38th Army captures Vinnitsa.
21 March	1st Ukrainian Front (1TA, 4TA) attacks and shatters the front between 1. Panzerarmee and 4. Panzerarmee.
22 March	The Stavka orders the 1st Ukrainian Front to complete the encirclement of the 1. Panzerarmee, while 2nd Ukrainian Front advances toward Romanian border.
23 March	Von Manstein orders Hube to shift his army westward to avoid encirclement.
	Tarnopol is encircled.
24 March	The 1TA reaches the Dniester near Gorodenka.
25 March	Proskurov is evacuated.
26 March	1st Ukrainian Front (4TA) captures Kamenets-Podolsky.
	Von Manstein orders Hube to break out to west, instead of southward.
	Luftflotte 4 begins airlift operations to 1. Panzerarmee.
28 March	Hube's 1. Panzerarmee begins attacking to the west.
29 March	Korpsgruppe Chevallerie reaches Skala-Podilska on the Zbruch River.
29 March	1TA captures Chernovtsy after three days of fighting.
31 March	Hitler relieves von Manstein of command and replaces him with Model.
2 April	Heeresgruppe Nordukraine is formed under Model.
4 April	Hube's Panzers reach Chortkov.
6 April	Hube's vanguard establishes contact with II SS-Panzerkorps.
16 April	The German garrison in Tarnopol is annihilated.
20 April	The last elements of 1. Panzerarmee cross the Strypa River.

OPPOSING COMMANDERS

GERMAN

Although the Oberkommando des Heeres (OKH) was nominally responsible for the Eastern Front, in fact Adolf Hitler micromanaged day-to-day military operations, often directing units down to individual divisions. During the Kamenets-Podolsky campaign, Hitler was located at Berchtesgaden or nearby Klessheim Castle. He was capable of relieving commanders he believed were disobeying his intent to hold fast on the Eastern Front, and he exerted a baleful influence upon all decision-making in Heeresgruppe Süd (Army Group South).

Generalfeldmarschall Erich Von Manstein (1887–1973), commander of Heeresgruppe Süd since February 1943. Von Manstein was one of the Wehrmacht's best operational-level planners, and it was his concept that led to a rapid German victory over France in 1940. As a field commander, von Manstein proved quite capable when provided with well-equipped and full-strength formations. He successfully commanded a motorized corps during the initial stages of Operation *Barbarossa* in 1941, and then, as commander of the 11. Armee in 1942, he achieved major victories at Sevastopol and Leningrad. Hitler initially regarded von Manstein as something of a military genius and that he could accomplish any task assigned. Consequently, when the Stalingrad crisis erupted in November 1942, Hitler appointed von Manstein head of Heeresgruppe Don and bade him to restore the situation. Von Manstein managed to prevent a complete collapse of the German southern front, but he could not save the trapped 6. Armee. In March 1943, von Manstein's successful counterattack at Kharkov – using SS-Obergruppenführer Paul Hausser's full-strength II SS-Panzerkorps – added further lustre to his military reputation. However, von Manstein's direction of Heeresgruppe Süd during the Battle of Kursk in July 1943 was marred by poor planning and overconfidence, which led to failure. Indeed, von Manstein's decline as a commander began in the aftermath of Kursk, when he failed to anticipate the timing or ferocity of the Soviet counteroffensive, which shattered his army group and hurled it back to the Dnepr. Von Manstein often underestimated his Soviet opponents, which led to the loss of Kiev, then the near-fiasco in the Korsun Pocket. He also became increasingly at odds with Hitler, who refused to consider withdrawals until forced by enemy advances. For his part, von Manstein demanded greater autonomy and

Generalfeldmarschall Erich von Manstein, commander of Heeresgruppe Süd. Von Manstein's operational brilliance was undermined by his inability to anticipate Zhukov or to retain Hitler's confidence, which left his command vulnerable and under-resourced. (Author)

more replacements, which Hitler was loath to provide. Consequently, by the start of the Kamenets-Podolsky campaign, von Manstein no longer had Hitler's confidence and was increasingly at a loss about how to conduct effective operations with the depleted and under-resourced formations under his command.

General der Panzertruppen HUBE

Generaloberst Hans-Valentin Hube (1890–1944), commander of the 1. Panzerarmee since October 1943. Hube was commissioned as an infantry officer in the Kaiser's Army and served on the Western Front throughout World War I. In September 1914, Hube was wounded and had his lower left arm amputated, but he returned to the front in 1915 and led an infantry battalion during the battles of the Somme (1916) and Cambrai (1917). Despite his injury, Hube was retained in the post-war Reichswehr, and he rose steadily through the infantry branch. He led an infantry regiment in the 1939 Polish campaign and an infantry division in the 1940 French campaign. Hube's division was converted into the 16. Panzer-Division, which he commanded during *Barbarossa* in 1941. In 1942, Hube's division was the first German formation to reach the Volga River at Stalingrad. During the Battle of Stalingrad, Hube was promoted to commander of the XIV Panzerkorps and repeatedly smashed Zhukov's counterattacks in the Kotluban sector. When the 6. Armee was surrounded by the Soviet Winter Counteroffensive, Hitler ordered Hube to fly out of the pocket to avoid capture. Hitler then sent Hube and the re-formed XIV Panzerkorps to Sicily, where he fought a masterful delaying action against Anglo-American forces in July 1943. Hube was an aggressive, competent, hands-on commander who excelled in tough situations.

Generaloberst Hans-Valentin Hube, commander of the 1. Panzerarmee. Hube was exactly the kind of commander that the Ostheer needed to survive in 1944 – tough, adaptable and capable of leading his troops under the most extreme conditions. (Bundesarchiv, Bild 146-2009-0114)

General der Infanterie Kurt von der Chevallerie (1891–1945), commander of the LIX Armeekorps since December 1941. Von der Chevallerie was a professional Prussian infantry officer, with a wealth of combat experience from both World War I and the Russian front in 1941–43. As a corps commander, he played a major role in the attempted relief of the Velikiye Luki garrison in the winter of 1942–43. Yet like many German commanders, von der Chevallerie tended to underestimate Soviet capabilities, which could lead to serious tactical mistakes.

General der Infanterie Kurt von der Chevallerie, commander of the LIX Armeekorps. Von der Chevallerie had to bear the brunt of Zhukov's initial offensive attacks, then create a viable perimeter, then lead the breakout operation to the west. It was a heavy responsibility for any commander and von der Chevallerie accomplished each task. (Author)

General der Panzertruppen Hermann Breith (1892–1964), commander of the III Panzerkorps since January 1943. Starting his military career as an infantry officer in 1911, Breith saw considerable combat on both the Eastern and Western Fronts in World War I. After the war, he was retained in the Reichswehr, and in 1925 he was transferred to the motor transport troops, which were covertly involved in creating a German armoured force. In 1935, Breith was given command of one of the first Panzer-Abteilungen (tank battalions), followed by command of a regiment in 1938 and a brigade in 1940. Breith led his Panzers in the Polish, Belgian and French campaigns. During the Moscow campaign in 1941, Breith led the 3. Panzer-Division to the outskirts of Tula. In 1942, Breith led his division during the Battle of Kharkov and the Caucasus campaign, until being sent into the Führer Reserve in October. Breith was given command of the III Panzerkorps, which he led during the Battle of Kursk, the retreat to the Dnepr and the Battle of the Korsun Pocket. Breith was one of the most experienced and intelligent German armour commanders in World War II, capable of getting the most out of the limited resources left to the Wehrmacht in 1944.

SOVIET

Soviet military operations were planned by the Stavka in Moscow, with input from Josef Stalin, but day-to-day operational control was exercised at the front level.

By early 1944, the Red Army possessed a good number of veteran command cadre who had the skill to conduct large-scale combined arms warfare and achieve most of their objectives. All of the senior Soviet commanders in the Kamenets-Podolsky campaign were younger than their German opposites, which gave them a bit of an edge in terms of stamina. The decision-making process in the Red Army was more streamlined than it had been earlier in the war, although Stalin and local political commissars still had some influence over operational priorities and timetables.

Marshal Georgi K. Zhukov (1896–1974) took over command of the 1st Ukrainian Front on 1 March 1944, just four days before the start of the Proskurov–Chernovtsy offensive. Zhukov was conscripted into the Tsarist Army in 1915 and served briefly as a cavalry non-commissioned officer at the front in 1917. At the outbreak of the Russian Civil War, Zhukov joined the Red Army. Zhukov was intelligent and hard-working enough to rise steadily during the inter-war period, and he commanded a cavalry division in 1933–37. When his superior was eliminated during the Stalinist purges, Zhukov moved up to corps command. Zhukov's great moment came at the Battle of Khalkhin-Gol in August 1939, where he encircled and demolished a reinforced Japanese division. Thereafter, Zhukov's star was on the rise and Stalin appointed him army chief of staff in January 1941, even though Zhukov had no general staff training. When the German invasion began, Zhukov played a critical role in defending the approaches to Leningrad, then rebuilding the shattered Western Front to save Moscow. Zhukov remained in command of the Western Front during 1942, mostly focused on trying

Marshal Georgi K. Zhukov was the primary author of the Kamenets-Podolsky campaign. In point of fact, Zhukov had not actually exercised direct field command for well over a year and took over the 1st Ukrainian Front only five days prior to the start of the offensive. Although familiar with the plan developed by Vatutin, he was less acquainted with the units under his command and their ability to accomplish their assigned missions. (Courtesy of the Central Museum of the Armed Forces, Moscow via Stavka)

to eliminate the German-held Rzhev salient but also playing an advisory role on the critical Stalingrad front. In August 1942, Stalin made Zhukov deputy commander-in-chief of the Red Army. Consequently, Zhukov was increasingly drawn into high-level operational planning in the Stavka and held no field commands in 1943, instead serving as a Stavka coordinator. When Vatutin was mortally wounded in February 1944, Zhukov stepped in to command the 1st Ukrainian Front. Zhukov was an expert at planning a set-piece battle, and he sought opportunities to encircle and destroy German forces. However, by 1944, Zhukov had transitioned into a 'big picture' officer, who was increasingly remote from tactical realities on the battlefield, particularly concerning weather, the enemy and the condition of Red Army units that had been in combat for months.

Marshal Ivan S. Konev (1897–1973), commander of the Steppe Front since July 1943 (which became the 2nd Ukrainian Front in October 1943). Konev came from a peasant background and was drafted into the Tsarist Army in 1916, serving briefly as an artilleryman against the Austro-Hungarians in Galicia. After the Tsarist collapse, Konev joined the Red Army and served as a commissar on an armoured train in the Far East. Although he attended the prestigious Frunze Military Academy, Konev spent a good portion of the inter-war period as a military commissar, and he assiduously worked his party connections to advance his career. Consequently, Konev survived the pre-war Stalinist purges unscathed, unlike many of his contemporaries. In 1941, Konev commanded the 19th Army at the Battle of Smolensk and was then given command of the Western Front in September. When the Western Front was demolished in the Vyazma-Bryansk catastrophe, Stalin wanted to liquidate Konev but was persuaded by Zhukov to give him another chance. Thereafter, Konev was assigned to command the Kalinin Front, which repeatedly failed to capture Rzhev in 1942. By 1943, Konev's reputation with Stalin was poor, but nevertheless Zhukov managed to get him assigned to command the Steppe Front for the Battle of Kursk. Konev's front played a critical role in the Soviet counteroffensive, which defeated the 4. Panzerarmee and recaptured Kharkov. During the subsequent Dnepr River campaign in October 1943, Konev turned in a competent performance, but his tendency to try to simultaneously accomplish multiple objectives prevented him from achieving a decisive success. Likewise, Konev's performance during the Battle of the Korsun Pocket was regarded by Stalin as less than satisfactory. However, Konev's front performed brilliantly in the opening stages of the Kamenets-Podolsky campaign, which probably irked Zhukov.

General-leytenant Mikhail Katukov (1900–76), commander of the 1st Tank Army since January 1943. Like Konev, Katukov came from a Russian peasant background, and he joined the Red Army in 1919. Katukov was commissioned as an infantry officer in 1922 and transitioned to mechanized forces in 1932. Dodging the purges, Katukov survived and was given command of a light tank brigade in 1938. When Germany invaded the Soviet Union, Katukov's first command was destroyed in the Battle of Dubno in June 1941, but he burnished his reputation by inflicting a

General-leytenant Mikhail Katukov, commander of the 1st Tank Army. One of the best of the senior Soviet armour leaders. (Author)

tactical setback upon Guderian's Panzers at the Battle of Mtsensk in October 1941. Katukov played a significant role in the Moscow counteroffensive and was rewarded with command of the 1st Tank Corps. As a corps commander, Katukov was defeated at Rzhev and Voronezh in 1942, but he proved capable of learning from his mistakes. Katukov was one of the most experienced and skilled Soviet senior armoured leaders, although he was not on par with the better German Panzer commanders like Breith.

General-leytenant Vasily M. Badanov (1895–1971), commander of the 4th Tank Army since July 1943. Badanov briefly served as a junior infantry officer in the Tsarist Army in 1917 before transitioning to the Red Army two years later. Badanov spent much of the inter-war period serving in the OGPU, the Soviet state security branch that replaced the Cheka. In 1932, Badanov received training in the armour branch, and in the turmoil that succeeded the Stalinist purges of the Red Army, he was given command of the 55th Tank Division in 1941. Badanov's division was destroyed in the Battle of Smolensk, but he proved competent enough to be given command of the 24th Tank Corps in early 1942. In December 1942, Badanov's tank corps conducted the successful Tatsinskaya Raid, which seriously disrupted German airlift operations to Stalingrad. However, Badanov withdrew the survivors of his corps without permission, and he was fortunate to avoid punishment for that transgression. In July 1943, Badanov's 4th Tank Army achieved a major breakthrough in Operation *Kutusov*, the Soviet counteroffensive, which led to the German evacuation of the Orel salient. Badanov was an intelligent and experienced senior armour leader who had demonstrated a flair for fast-paced mobile operations.

General-polkovnik Pavel S. Rybalko (1894–1948), commander of the 3rd Guards Tank Army since May 1943. Rybalko was an ethnic Ukrainian who was commissioned as an infantry officer in the Red Army in 1919. Although he transitioned to the cavalry branch after the Russian Civil War, Rybalko spent most of the inter-war period in a variety of special assignments, including intelligence work and as a military adviser in China. Rybalko sat out the first year of the German invasion in Moscow, as a staff officer. It was not until summer 1942 that Rybalko received his first major field assignment, as deputy commander of the newly formed 5th Tank Army, which abruptly ended when the formation was quickly demolished during the disastrous counterattack at Voronezh. Despite his limited command experience, Rybalko was assigned to lead the 3rd Tank Army (3TA) during the Soviet Winter Counteroffensive, and he achieved major victories in January–February 1943, first playing a major role in the destruction of the Hungarian 2nd Army and then in the liberation of Kharkov (Operation *Star*). However, von Manstein's 'Backhand Blow' counterattack retook Kharkov and defeated Rybalko's 3TA. Afterwards, Rybalko's command was re-formed as the 3rd Guards Tank Army (3GTA) and he led it during the Soviet counteroffensives around the Kursk salient in July 1943, then in the Dnepr operation, which led to the liberation of Kiev. Even by Soviet standards, Rybalko was noted for suffering excessive casualties and losing most of his tanks in the initial stages of breakthrough battles.

General-leytenant Vasily M. Badanov, commander of the 4th Tank Army. Badanov had proved himself capable in fast-moving mobile operations in 1942–43, and he would catch the Germans by surprise at Kamenets-Podolsky. However, he was badly wounded during a German counterattack and his overextended forces were left leaderless for several critical days. (Author)

OPPOSING PLANS

GERMAN

By early March 1944, the Third Reich had few – if any – realistic strategic options left, which made operational-level planning extremely difficult. In the East, Soviet armies had liberated most of Ukraine and had pushed von Manstein's Heeresgruppe Süd back to the Bug River. In the centre, the Soviets had taken Smolensk, and in the north, the Red Army had driven the Wehrmacht back from the outskirts of Leningrad. The Soviets now clearly held the strategic initiative and were steadily pushing westward, halted only occasionally by obstinate resistance at certain points. With the Third Reich's military fortunes in obvious decline, Hitler recognized that both Hungary and Romania were looking to negotiate separate peace deals before the Red Army reached their borders. Meanwhile in Italy, the Western Allies had landed at Anzio in January 1944 and threatened Rome. It was also evident that the Allies were preparing for a major cross-channel invasion of north-west Europe in the summer of 1944, which could open up a third front. Germany still had sufficient resources to effectively fight on one front, at least for a while, but not on multiple fronts. Thus, Germany had to carefully choose where to apply its limited resources in order to achieve the most strategic benefit, but Hitler and the OKH differed sharply on their view of priorities.

Seen through the professional military lenses employed by the OKH staff, the Eastern Front was clearly the main theatre of operations and that is where its Großer Generalstab-trained officers wanted priority of resources assigned. By withdrawing to shorter, well-prepared defensive lines and receiving the lion's share of replacements, the Ostheer (army in the East) might be able to stop the Red Army short of the German border. With luck, the Ostheer might even be able to mount a successful counteroffensive against an overextended Red Army, thereby gaining time for the Third Reich to recover some of its strength. On the other hand, the OKH regarded Italy as a secondary theatre that should be treated as an economy of force effort – only minimal resources should be expended. As for France, the OKH was justifiably concerned about an Allied invasion, but a successful defence in the East would free up some reserves to deal with that contingency. Essentially, the OKH was willing to accept higher risk in the west, in order to prioritize fending off the main threat that was already approaching Germany's eastern border regions. Nor was the OKH eager to expend much military resource keeping Hungary and

The strategic situation in south-west Ukraine, 1 March 1944

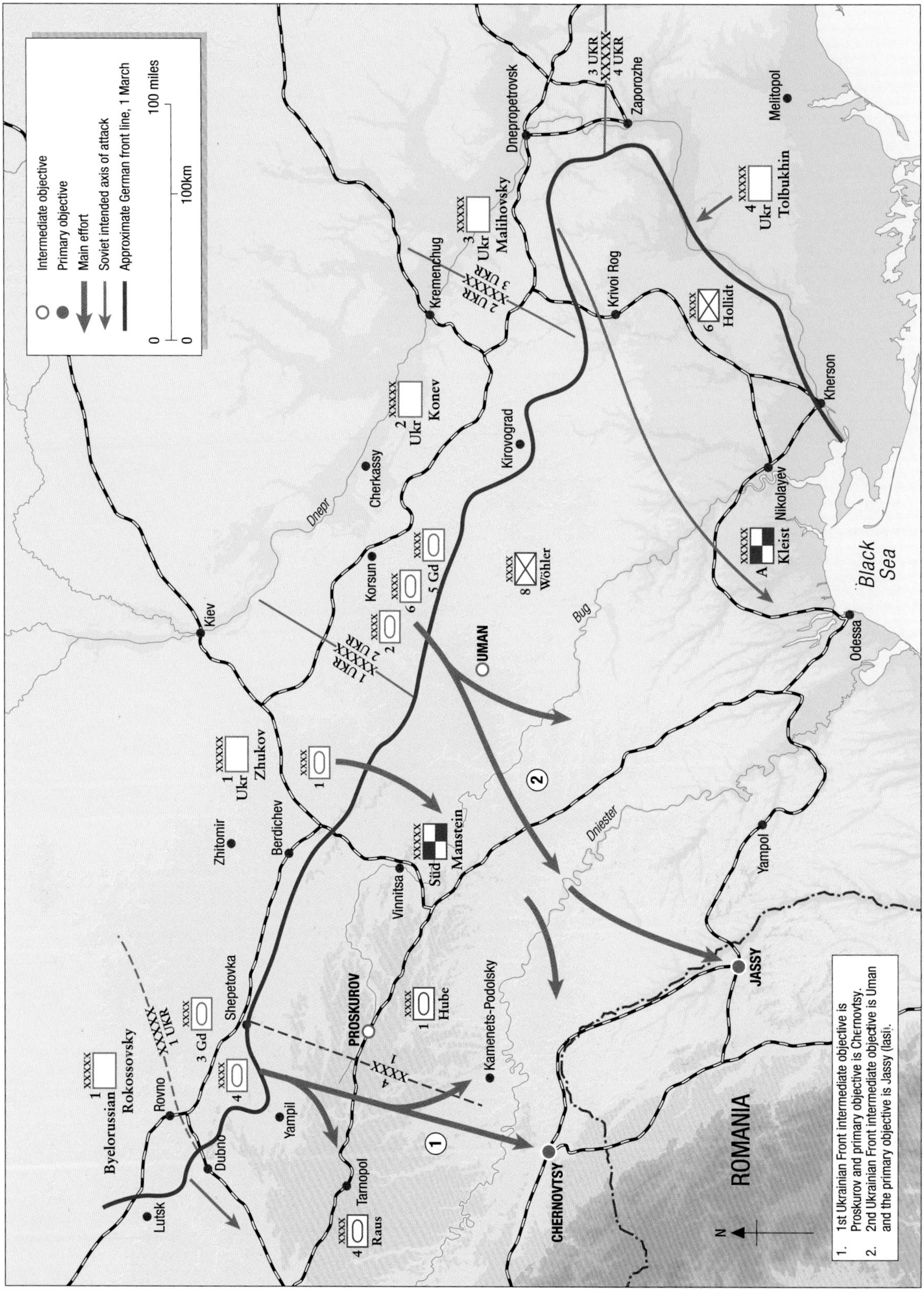

Legend:
- ○ Intermediate objective
- ● Primary objective
- ↓ Main effort
- ↓ Soviet intended axis of attack
- ⌁⌁ Approximate German front line, 1 March

Scale: 100 miles / 100km

Units and locations (as labelled on map):

3 UKR XXXXX / 4 UKR — Zaporozhe
Dnepropetrovsk
Melitopol
4 Ukr Tolbukhin XXXX
3 Ukr Malinovsky XXXX
2 UKR XXXXX / 3 UKR
Kremenchug
Krivoi Rog
6 Hollidt XXXX
Kherson
2 Ukr Konev XXXX
Kirovograd
Cherkassy
Dnepr
Black Sea
8 Wöhler XXXX
Bug
A Kleist XXXX — Nikolayev
Odessa
5 Gd XXXX / 6 XXXX — Korsun
Kiev
2 XXXX / 1 UKR XXXXX / 2 UKR
UMAN ○
1 Ukr Zhukov XXXXX
1 XXXX
Zhitomir
Berdichev
Vinnitsa
Süd Manstein XXXXX
Dniester
Yampol
1 Byelorussian Rokossovsky XXXXX — Rovno
3 Gd XXXX / 1 UKR XXXXX — Shepetovka
Lutsk
Dubno
Yampil
4 XXXX
Tarnopol
4 Raus XXXX
PROSKUROV ●
1 Hube XXXX
Kamenets-Podolsky
4 XXXX / I
CHERNOVTSY ●
JASSY ●
ROMANIA

Numbered notes box:

1. 1st Ukrainian Front intermediate objective is Proskurov and primary objective is Chernovtsy.
2. 2nd Ukrainian Front intermediate objective is Uman and the primary objective is Jassy (Iasi).

N ↓

Romania in the war, since their battlefield contributions to date had afforded very little benefit to Germany's war effort.

In contrast, Hitler looked at the war primarily through political and ideological lenses. He regarded German national morale and support for his regime as the *sine qua non* for successful prosecution of the war. Hitler remembered from World War I that continuous German withdrawals and defecting allies had been the precursor for regime collapse, so he vehemently opposed both. After the unexpected debacles of 1941–43, he also regarded the Eastern Front as something of a bottomless pit for German resources. Despite receiving large numbers of the best troops and equipment that the Third Reich possessed, von Manstein's Heeresgruppe Süd had been consistently outmanoeuvred and defeated since July 1943. Although Hitler usually opposed withdrawals on the Eastern Front, he also recognized that there was far more prestige in holding Paris or Rome, as opposed to obscure Ukrainian towns. Consequently, Hitler directed the OKH to send over 500 tanks and assault guns to Italy in January–February 1944 to launch a ferocious counterattack against the Anzio beachhead, in the hope of gaining a cheap prestige victory. The Anzio counteroffensive came close to success, but ultimately tied down considerable German armoured units in a secondary theatre. Hitler also directed the OKH to assemble a large armoured reserve in France, amounting to well over 1,000 tanks and assault guns, to deal with the expected Allied invasion. In addition, about one-third of new tank production was earmarked for the Western Front, which further starved the Ostheer of replacements at a critical moment. Furthermore, Hitler was adamant about keeping a mobile reserve to deal with any potential defection attempts by his allies, so the newly formed Panzer-Lehr Division (with 184 tank and assault guns) was kept near Vienna, along with several infantry divisions.

As a result of Hitler's skewed priorities, von Manstein and Hube were forced to 'make bricks without straw' – in other words, to try and create the impression of a strong front line to stop further Soviet advances, but without the necessary replacements. Von Manstein's left was held by Raus' 4. Panzerarmee, which was responsible for the area between Shepetovka and Rovno. Raus could not create anything like a continuous front line, and the XIII Armeekorps on his left, near Kovel, was forced to deploy SS-Polizei units to hold strongpoints. Indeed, in some places there were 500m

A platoon (Zug) of Panthers from the SS-*LSSAH* moving in column, early March 1944. After the conclusion of the Korsun Pocket relief operation, von Manstein quickly began redeploying his best Panzer units to sectors that were likely to be attacked next. Zhukov's offensive still caught the Germans off balance and in the midst of redistributing III Panzerkorps to reinforce the vulnerable boundary between the 1. Panzerarmee and 4. Panzerarmee. (Author)

between German-held positions and the so-called main line of resistance (*Hauptkampflinie* or HKL) was occupied just by support troops. Likewise, General der Panzertruppen Hermann Balck's XXXXVIII Panzerkorps maintained only a very tenuous connection with Hube's 1. Panzerarmee near Yampil. Hube's situation was somewhat better, in that he was able to create a nearly continuous front between Shepetovka and Uman (a distance of about 150km) and maintain a small reserve with III Panzerkorps. The OKH even managed to send Hube the 96. Infanterie-Division, transferred piecemeal from Heeresgruppe Nord in February. On the army group's right flank, General der Infanterie Otto Wöhler's 8. Armee defended the sector from Uman toward the area south-east of Kirovograd. Aside from Raus' dangling left flank, the obvious threat was posed by the Soviet-held salient near Yampil, which created a large bulge in von Manstein's front at the boundary between the 4. Panzerarmee and 1. Panzerarmee; a breakthrough here would quickly threaten the key rail junction at Tarnopol.

Anticipating that Zhukov would make his main effort in the Yampil sector, von Manstein began repositioning his meagre armoured reserves in late February to counter the expected enemy course of action. The 6. Panzer-Division, SS-*Das Reich* and *LSSAH* were ordered to move to backstop the LIX Armeekorps defences around the Yampil bulge and to shield Tarnopol, while the 1. And 19. Panzer-Divisionen reinforced the Shepetovka sector. Raus was ordered to transfer the 7. Panzer-Division from the XIII Armeekorps sector to provide a tactical reserve near Tarnopol. While these adjustments succeeded in reinforcing the sectors where Zhukov intended to make his main effort, they reduced the ability of Breith's III Panzerkorps to control its now dispersed armour and seriously weakened Hube's right flank boundary with the 8. Armee.

Hitler optimistically hoped that adverse weather and supply difficulties might delay Zhukov's next offensive, but ordered von Manstein to hold his ground whenever the enemy attacked. Unsatisfied with von Manstein's preference for 'mobile defence' to conserve his units, Hitler decided to further complicate Heeresgruppe Süd's already constricted options by mandating the use of hedgehog-style defences known as Fortified Areas (*feste Plätze*) to slow enemy offensives. Consequently, Yampil was designated as a *fester Platz* and part of the 6. SS-Freiwilligen-Sturmbrigade *Langemarck* was assigned to hold it. From the Ostheer's perspective, these Fortified Areas were 'die-in-place' missions that would uselessly sacrifice troops and negatively impact front-line morale for very limited benefit. Von Manstein and his subordinate commanders tried to avoid the Fortified Area mandate as much as possible, but each subterfuge employed further increased Hitler's mistrust of his front-line commanders.

A Panther tank at a railhead, surrounded by apparently empty 200-litre fuel drums. Although equipped with an excellent main gun and sloped armour, the Panther was a fuel hog that required 730 litres to move 100km under ideal conditions. The thick mud in Ukraine typically reduced the Panther's range to just 50–60km on a full load of fuel. (Author)

The mud in Ukraine – Napoleon's 'fifth element' – greatly influenced mobile operations for both sides during the Kamenets-Podolsky campaign. In addition to slowing movement, the thick, sticky mud tended to wear out vehicle running gear, as well as final drives on tanks. (Author)

SOVIET

By mid-February 1944, Soviet armies had ground to a halt across virtually the entire Eastern Front, due to supply shortages, mud and heavy losses. During this brief pause, the Stavka considered its next set of operational objectives. Marshal Zhukov, in Moscow during this period, played a major role in the planning process, along with Marshal Aleksandr M. Vasilevskiy and General Aleksei I. Antonov from the General Staff. The Stavka's foremost priority was to complete the eviction of all Axis forces from the western Ukraine and the Crimea. The loss of the last Axis positions in Ukraine was expected to precipitate the defection of Hungary and Romania, further weakening the German position in the East. Once these military-political objectives were attained, the Red Army could then apply all its resources toward a direct advance upon Warsaw, followed by Berlin. The Stavka provided initial planning guidance to Vatutin's 1st Ukrainian Front on 18 February, and he was allotted just five days to develop an operational plan for an offensive involving eight armies. Given the stakes involved, the Stavka decided to ensure success by committing all six available tank armies to the Ukrainian operation; the 1st Ukrainian Front would get three tank armies (1TA, 3GTA and 4TA) and the 2nd Ukrainian Front would get the other three (2TA, 5GTA, 6TA).

Soviet replacement tanks and troops move toward the front in anticipation of the next offensive, early 1944. The Stavka's ability to keep feeding in men and materiel from its strategic reserve (RVGK) enabled Zhukov to keep the pressure on von Manstein's Heeresgruppe Süd. (Author)

On 25 February 1944, the Stavka approved Vatutin's plan for the offensive, which was scheduled to begin one week later. Despite the fact that the Soviet field armies were nearly exhausted and operating on a logistical shoestring, the Stavka developed a rather grandiose operational concept that envisioned a coordinated offensive by no less than four fronts. A new front, designated as the 2nd Belorussian Front,

was formed on 17 February from three of Vatutin's armies in the Rovno–Lutsk sector and assigned the task of attacking due west toward Kovel – against 4. Panzerarmee's dangling left flank. Vatutin's 1st Ukrainian Front would attack in the Yampil–Shepetovka sector with the objective of slicing through Raus' right flank and then advancing to cross the Dniester River and seizing Chernovtsy. Konev's 2nd Ukrainian Front would advance from Zvenigorodka to smash the junction between the 1. Panzerarmee and 8. Armee, then advancing to capture Uman and Jassy in Romania. On the left, the 3rd Ukrainian Front would advance due south to Odessa on the Black Sea. The grand Soviet offensive would begin on the right, in southern Belorussia, with each front attacking one day after its neighbour on the right. The Stavka expected this series of powerful hammer blows to shatter the Axis front in multiple places and demolish von Manstein's Heeresgruppe Süd. Any Axis fragments that survived the initial onslaught would be pushed back into Hungary or Romania, which were expected to opt out of the war at that point. However, the Soviet March offensive in Ukraine was based on a number of assumptions about how the enemy would react, which might not prove correct.

In order to prepare for the March offensive, Rybalko's 3GTA had to be shifted to the Yampil bulge and Badanov's 4th Tank Army had to move to the Shepetovka sector from the Stavka Reserve (RVGK), a distance of 350km. Zhukov's main effort would be made in the Yampil–Shepetovka sector, where General-polkovnik Andrei A. Grechko's 1st Guards Army and General-polkovnik Ivan D. Cherniakhovsky's 60th Army were expected to breach the German LIX Armeekorps front with a massive assault. Once the enemy front was breached, the 3GTA and 4TA would advance quickly to exploit the situation and drive south to create a deep wedge between the 4. Panzerarmee and 1. Panzerarmee. Prior to the main attack on 4 March, the 1st Ukrainian Front mounted local attacks on nearly a daily basis in order to keep the Germans off balance and aggressively probe for weak spots.

A Soviet truck crosses an improvised bridge over a frozen river. Soviet front-level logistics were severely constrained during the Kamenets-Podolsky campaign, forcing Zhukov's front-line units to operate on a hand-to-mouth basis for ammunition and fuel. The Stavka's decision to conduct back-to-back offensives prevented the accumulation of any significant logistic stockpiles during the winter of 1943–44. (From the fonds of the RGAKFD in Krasnogorsk via Stavka)

OPPOSING FORCES

GERMAN

In early March 1944, Generaloberst Hans-Valentin Hube's 1. Panzerarmee consisted of 18 divisions (eight Panzer, one Panzergrenadier, eight infantry and one artillery) with a total of roughly 220,000 troops. The four subordinate corps were the III, XXIV and XXXXVI Panzerkorps and the LIX Armeekorps. A number of German units were being transferred to the control of the XXXXVIII Panzerkorps in the 4. Panzerarmee at the start of Zhukov's March offensive and these units would return to 1. Panzerarmee control during the campaign. Raus' 4. Panzerarmee played a major role at the start of the Kamenets-Podolsky campaign, but Zhukov's offensive shattered it into fragments.

Panzer units

Of the 24 Panzer-Divisionen deployed on the Eastern Front in March 1944, eight were assigned to Hube's 1. Panzerarmee (three were with the 4. Panzerarmee and four with the 8. Armee). On paper, Hube should have had over 1,000 tanks and assault guns in his command, but in reality he had fewer than 900 – and only one-third were operational. Due to shortages of spare parts and major assemblies – particularly final drives – the 1. Panzerarmee had a huge backlog of armoured fighting vehicles (AFVs) awaiting repairs in depots at Uman and Proskurov. By early 1944, a Panzer-Division was authorized a nominal strength of about 14,000 troops, with its primary fighting components consisting of a Panzer Regiment with either one or two Panzer-Abteilungen (one equipped with 80–95 PzKpfw IV tanks, the other with 76 PzKpfw V Panther tanks), four Panzergrenadier battalions (one mounted in SPW half-tracks), two motorized or self-propelled artillery battalions, one armoured reconnaissance battalion and one Panzerjäger-Bataillon (with 14 Marder II/III tank destroyers). In theory, the Panzer-Division, equipped with up to 160 tanks and 300 other AFVs, was capable of serving as a powerful, mobile strike force. Yet in reality, Hube's worn-down Panzer-Divisionen in early March 1944 were operating with barely 10–20 per cent of their authorized number of AFVs and combat troops. Of the eight Panther-Abteilungen available to the 1. Panzerarmee at the beginning of March 1944, they possessed a total of only 55 operational Panthers, with another 190 under repair, out of a total authorized strength of 608 Panthers. The most combat-effective units were the 1., 6., and

By this point of the war on the Eastern Front, it was common for the Germans to employ mixed Kampfgruppen with both PzKpfw IV and Panther tanks. This group is probably from the 1. Panzer-Division. (Fotoarchiv für Zeitgeschichte/Archiv/Süddeutsche Zeitung Photo)

7. Panzer-Divisionen and the 1. SS-Panzer-Division *LSSAH*, each of which was fortunate to operate 20–30 tanks on a good day. On 3 March, the 1. Panzer-Division had just arrived near Proskurov after a 200km road march, and 50 per cent of its motor vehicles were non-operational and one artillery battalion was immobilized for lack of prime movers.

Hube's 1. Panzerarmee also included several other types of armoured formations, including elements of two schwere Panzer-Abteilungen (Heavy Tank Battalions), which were army-level assets (*Heerestruppen*), nominally equipped with 45 PzKpfw VI Tiger tanks. In addition, there were several self-propelled schwere Panzerjäger Abteilungen (Heavy Anti-tank Battalions), equipped with either Marder II/III or Hornisse tank destroyers. Although originally created solely to support the infantry, Sturmartillerie units had evolved into multi-purpose AFVs that were increasingly used in the anti-tank role as substitutes for tanks. Hube's 1. Panzerarmee had four independent Sturmgeschütz-Abteilungen (each nominally equipped with 22 StuG III assault guns and nine StuH 42 assault howitzers), as well as some smaller detachments integrated into various divisions. Just prior to the start of Zhukov's March offensive, the 20. Panzergrenadier-Division was fortunate to receive 42 new StuG III assault guns.

The majority of the 1. Panzerarmee's operational armoured force consisted of four types of AFVs: about 100 PzKpfw IV Ausf H medium tanks, 55 PzKpfw V Panther Ausf A medium tanks, about 50 PzKpfw VI Tigers and roughly 100 StuG III Ausf G or StuG IV assault guns. While the Tiger and Panther were formidable tanks with impressive long-range firepower, their bulk made it difficult for them to cross standard pontoon bridges over the numerous water obstacles in the western Ukraine. Both tanks were designed to operate with significant logistic support, particularly in terms of maintenance and spare parts – which were inadequate even before the 1. Panzerarmee was isolated. Furthermore, the off-road fuel-consumption of the gas-guzzling Tigers (6.75 litres/km) and Panthers (7.3 litres/km) also became a major problem once the 1. Panzerarmee had to be supplied by air. In the thick Ukrainian mud, the Panther and Tiger could barely move 50–60km on a full load of fuel. In contrast, the PzKpfw IV Ausf H tank and StuG III Ausf G assault guns could cross the available pontoon bridges and consumed only half as much fuel as the German heavy tanks. German Panzer and Sturmartillerie crews still enjoyed an advantage in training, but combat losses were gradually dulling their former tactical edge. The AFVs in 1. Panzerarmee were vital to the survival and breakout of Hube's isolated army, but their combat effectiveness could not be sustained for long by an airlift.

Infantry

The Ostheer's infantry units were in an advanced state of decline by March 1944 due to the inability of the OKH to fully replace losses in men and equipment. In October 1943, the OKH directed a reorganization of the infantry division structure (*neue Art*) to recognize that fact, by reducing all infantry regiments from three to two battalions. The new infantry division had an authorized strength of about 12,700 men, although there was considerable variance in front-line units. Along with six infantry battalions, the new structure created a Fusilier-Bataillon and a Feldersatz-Bataillon (FEB) to train new replacements in situ. While the authorized strength for an infantry battalion was just over 700 troops, actual numbers in the battalions in the 1. Panzerarmee in early March 1944 ranged between 100 and 400 men, with the average strength being around 200 men. A few of Hube's infantry divisions retained some combat effectiveness, but others, such as the 34., 82. and 198. Infanterie-Divisionen were burnt-out wrecks with just 20 per cent of their authorized infantry strength remaining. In order to compensate for reduced manpower, the German infantry regiments were provided with a variety of new weapons to enhance their defensive firepower, particularly against Soviet tanks. Strenuous efforts were made to boost the infantry's organic anti-tank capabilities; battalions were provided with the 8.8cm Panzerschreck rocket launcher and the disposable Panzerfaust anti-tank rocket, while regiments were provided with three 7.5cm Pak 40 anti-tank guns. At division-level, additional Pak 40s, StuG III assault guns or Marder II/III tank destroyers added further anti-tank firepower. German infantry battalions also saw improvements in their indirect firepower support, by the addition of four 12cm Granatwerfer 42 mortars, while divisions retained their artillery regiments (with 36 10.5cm and nine 15cm howitzers). However, additional firepower assets could not make up for the heavy losses in veteran junior officers and NCOs, who were the backbone of Ostheer infantry units. In order to accelerate the number of replacements sent to the Ostheer, German infantry training was reduced to eight weeks. The new recruits arrived at the front unprepared for high-intensity combat operations and proved less effective and motivated than their predecessors, which exacerbated the downward spiral.

Altogether, Hube's 1. Panzerarmee had about 72 'leg' infantry battalions, which had limited tactical mobility and were now suited only to defensive missions. It is noteworthy that during the recent Korsun Pocket relief operation, no German infantry division had played a prominent role. In addition, the Panzer formations in Hube's army included 46 Panzergrenadier-Bataillone, seven of which were nominally *gepanzert* (armoured infantry) battalions mounted in SPW half-tracks. However, since Hube's army possessed only about 245 operational SPW at the start of the campaign, this meant that even the *gepanzert* battalions had no more than 40 per cent of their authorized transport. Likewise, the motorized infantry battalions were

A German machine gunner equipped with the formidable MG 42. Although these troops have the look of veterans, many of the replacements reaching the Ostheer by March 1944 were hastily trained teenagers or rear echelon troops redesignated as infantry. (Nik Cornish at www.stavka.photos)

A pair of German Wespe (Sd.Kfz. 124) self-propelled howitzers. By mounting a 10.5cm howitzer on a PzKpfw II chassis, the Wehrmacht created a highly effective fire support platform for Panzer Kampfgruppen. Typically, each Panzer-Division was supposed to have two batteries of Wespe, each equipped with six firing vehicles and two ammunition resupply vehicles. (Nik Cornish at www.stavka.photos)

hobbled by the fact that many of the trucks used by the Ostheer had limited off-road mobility in mud and thousands of trucks were sidelined awaiting repairs. Even in elite units like the *LSSAH*, over 1,500 trucks were non-operational at the end of February 1944 and its Panzergrenadier-Bataillone reported that they possessed only 30 per cent mobility. The Panzergrenadier-Bataillone were afforded some priority for replacements, but their average strength was just 250 men. For example, at the start of the campaign, Major Paul Stahl's I./Panzergrenadier-Regiment 114. 114 in 6. Panzer-Division had a combat strength of only 309 of its 903 authorized troops (35 per cent), 30 of its 80 machine guns and half its 8cm mortars. In German military doctrine, infantry was supposed to be a critical part of the combined arms team in both offensive and defensive missions, but by March 1944, most *Ostheer* infantry units were little more than line-holders. While the Panzergrenadier units in the Panzer-Divisionen still had the mobility and firepower to make a difference on the battlefield, even they were in decline due to losses in manpower and equipment.

Logistics

Prior to Zhukov's March 1944 offensive, Hube's 1. Panzerarmee relied upon the double-track line from Lvov through Tarnopol, Proskurov and Vinnitsa as its primary line of communications. Although it was possible to move some supplies by road from Hungary over the Dniester River, this was an inadequate alternative. Overall, Hube's army required an absolute minimum of 535 tons per day of ammunition and fuel (not including food or medical supplies) just to conduct ordinary defensive operations. By March 1944, most Ostheer units were plagued with chronic shortages of fuel and ammunition, which significantly reduced their combat effectiveness. The situation improved somewhat as Heeresgruppe Süd withdrew closer to its main supply bases in Uman, Proskurov and Vinnitsa, but the sudden loss of depots proved catastrophic. Furthermore, the Ostheer's over-reliance on horse-drawn transport, particularly for the infantry and artillery, seriously impaired its logistic sustainability.

Luftwaffe

Generalleutnant Hans Seidemann's VIII Fliegerkorps was responsible for providing air support to Hube's 1. Panzerarmee, although its capabilities were rather limited. In particular, Seidemann had only a single Jagdgruppe (fighter group) equipped with Bf 109G fighters, which made it impossible to secure the airspace over Hube's sector. Nevertheless, Seidemann did have some significant close air support assets with Schlachtgeschwader 77 (SG 77) and Schlachtgeschwader 9 (SG 9), which altogether possessed over 100 Stukas and fighter-bombers. Under the right conditions, the venerable Ju 87D Stuka proved that it could still provide valuable support to ground troops, at least when Soviet fighters were absent. Endemic fuel shortages were also beginning to cramp Luftwaffe air operations. While the Ostheer welcomed close air support when it could get it, the Luftwaffe's most important contribution to the army by this point in the war was aerial resupply. Seidemann's VIII Fliegerkorps had three transport groups equipped with Ju 52s, another group utilizing He 111 bombers and a glider unit equipped with DFS 230 gliders. Even better, Generalmajor Fritz Morzik was the Lufttransportchef (air transport chief) for the VIII Fliegerkorps; Morzik and his veteran staff had organized the Demyansk and Stalingrad airlift operations in 1942, then the Korsun airlift in February 1944. As a result, the Luftwaffe airlift capability was actually becoming more efficient and more agile due to learning from past mistakes, which enabled it to better serve the needs of encircled forces.

SOVIET

In early March 1944, Zhukov's 1st Ukrainian Front had three tank armies and four combined arms armies, totalling about 800,000 personnel. Only part of Konev's 2nd Ukrainian Front was directly involved in operations against Hube's 1. Panzerarmee, but this still amounted to two tank armies and one combined arms army, equivalent to about 200,000 personnel. Thus, in rough numbers, the Red Army headed into the Proskurov–Chernovtsy offensive with a 4:1 numerical advantage in manpower.

Armour

Zhukov had a nearly unprecedented amount of armour available under his command for the upcoming offensive, consisting of no less than three tank armies (1TA, 3GTA, 4TA); altogether these three tank armies comprised six tank corps, three mechanized corps, two independent tank brigades and five independent heavy tank regiments. Konev's armoured spearhead (2TA, 6TA) added another three tank corps and one mechanized corps, plus several independent units.

On paper, the Soviet tank corps of late 1943 were each authorized 208 T-34/76 medium tanks, usually two self-propelled gun regiments (with 21 SU-76 and 16 SU-85 or 12 SU-152 assault guns), six battalions of motorized infantry and a total of around 11,000 personnel. The mechanized corps were larger formations, with about 16,000 personnel, 183 T-34 tanks, 40–60 assault guns and ten battalions of motorized infantry. The only serious weakness in the Soviet tank and motorized corps was the limited amount of organic artillery fire support and other support units. Although Zhukov used all his influence with the Stavka to replace

Soviet infantry, winter 1943–44. Morale among front-line troops was improving, despite continued heavy losses, because it was apparent that victory was approaching. Many of Zhukov's newest recruits were Ukrainian, pressed into Red Army service after the liberation of Kiev. (From the fonds of the RGAKFD in Krasnogorsk via Stavka)

Soviet '*Desantniki*' infantry rode tanks into battle; in this case, it seems that one squad is mounted on each T-34. This tactic ensured that armoured spearheads always had some infantry support with them, but it led to very heavy casualties among the exposed troops. Furthermore, the fighting efficiency of the tank crew was hindered by having infantrymen covering sights and generally getting in the way. (Courtesy of the Central Museum of the Armed Forces, Moscow via Stavka)

the losses suffered in the January–February fighting, in early March 1944 his armoured armada was at less than 50 per cent of authorized strength, with only about 1,100 operational tanks and 200+ self-propelled guns. Konev's armoured forces were even more depleted; for example, Bogdanov's 2nd Tank Army had only 35 per cent of its AFVs operational, amounting to 175 tanks and 65 self-propelled guns. Nevertheless, the Red Army enjoyed at least a 5:1 numerical superiority in AFVs over Hube's 1. Panzerarmee at the start of March 1944. Furthermore, Soviet tank units now had a solid core of experienced veterans, which made them much more tactically competitive against the German Panzer units.

In early 1944, the primary Soviet tank was the T-34/76 Model 1943, which came in a variety of sub-models. While often undermined by quality control issues due to hasty manufacturing procedures, the T-34/76 Model 1943 was still a well-rounded tank that was suited to high-operations tempo manoeuvre warfare. Thanks to its proven diesel engine, the T-34/76 could move over 100km across muddy terrain, or about 150km with external fuel tanks – double the typical operational range of the PzKpfw IV tank in Ukrainian conditions. When equipped with improved APBC or APCR ammunition, the T-34/76 could engage the Panther with some chance of success, particularly with flank shots. Nevertheless, the Soviet State Defence Committee (GKO) recognized that the T-34/76 was seriously outgunned by the better-armed German Panther and Tiger heavy tanks, so it pushed for the rapid adoption of a variety of new AFVs that could defeat the enemy's heavy tanks. The first to appear was the SU-152, armed with the 152mm ML-20S howitzer, which performed well at the Battle of Kursk in July 1943 and was then superseded by the improved ISU-152 in December 1943. However, the 152mm howitzer was in low-rate production, so few were available to equip assault guns. Furthermore, the heavy 152mm howitzer had a very low rate of fire and each assault gun equipped with it could carry only a maximum of 20 rounds of ammunition. Consequently, the GKO placed its emphasis on AFVs armed with the 85mm D-5T gun, which resulted in the SU-85 assault gun entering service in August 1943, then the KV-85 and IS-1 heavy tanks in November 1943. The D-5T gun could penetrate the Tiger tank's thick armour at 1,000m. By April 1944, the new IS-2 heavy tank (armed with the 122mm D-25T gun) would begin reaching the 1st Ukrainian Front, albeit in small quantities at first.

Rifle troops

Zhukov had 39 rifle divisions at his disposal for the next offensive and Konev would commit another nine rifle divisions against Hube. Of these divisions, only six were better-equipped Guards units (four in the 1st Ukrainian Front). The Soviet rifle division of 1943 was organized around three rifle regiments and an artillery regiment (20 76mm guns and 12 122mm howitzers), with an aggregate authorized strength of 9,300 troops. In reality, the rifle divisions in the 1st and 2nd Ukrainian Fronts in March 1944 were typically at 50 per cent of authorized strength due to heavy losses, while the handful of Guards rifle divisions were usually closer to 70 per cent of authorized strength. Unlike the Germans, the Soviets could still replace their infantry losses fairly quickly through the simple expedient of conscripting every military-age male they came across as they advanced westward. Since the fall of Kiev, the Red Army had been able to scoop up about 200,000 Ukrainian replacements. In February 1944, Moskalenko's 38th Army was provided with 24,000 replacements. However, these hastily conscripted troops had minimal training and were oftentimes little more than cannon fodder in their first campaign. Leytenant Evgeni Bessonov, a motorized infantry platoon leader in the 6th Guards Mechanized Corps, stated that the Ukrainian conscripts tended to be over 40, untrained and timid in action.

A single Soviet rifle division had very limited offensive capability, but it was standard doctrine by this point to mass the best available troops from several divisions in a rifle corps to form a 'shock group', with artillery and engineer support. The best-equipped shock groups were also provided with a separate self-propelled gun regiment, equipped with 16–21 SU-76 assault guns. Soviet shock groups were intended to create breaches in the enemy front-line defences in order to create a corridor for the tank corps to exploit through. After that, rifle divisions were expected to protect the flanks of the advance, help contain enemy counterattacks and reduce bypassed enemy units. About 20 per cent of the Soviet rifle troops – those brigades within tank or mechanized corps – were motorized and capable of keeping up with the armoured advance. The remainder of the Soviet rifle troops plodded along behind, on foot.

Artillery and support troops

Unlike the Germans, who decentralized their artillery in order to provide each division with adequate firepower support, the Red Army centralized most of its artillery in army- and front-level formations. Zhukov had two artillery divisions supporting the 1st Guards Army and one supporting the 60th Army. The 17th Artillery Division was the strongest formation and was authorized over 350 guns and mortars (including 24 203mm howitzers). The Soviet artillerymen had learned that by massing fires from these divisions, they could blast just about any enemy defence to pieces, which forced German infantry units to further disperse for survivability – but dispersion made them even more vulnerable to Soviet tank attacks. Consequently, Soviet artillery had become the premier tool for creating the conditions for effective breakthrough attacks.

The NKO spent considerable effort boosting the capabilities of the Soviet engineer troops, in anticipation of crossing water obstacles as the Red Army advanced westward. Each of Zhukov's armies had at least one or two attached engineer battalions but the main river-crossing capabilities resided in front-level pontoon brigades and battalions. For example, an engineer battalion equipped with the DPM-42 pontoon system could provide a 50-ton bridge over a 70+ metre wide obstacle in just three to four hours. With the new TMP pontoon bridge, Soviet engineers gained the ability to construct 100-ton capacity bridges over much wider obstacles. Furthermore, the Soviet pontoon engineers were also capable of ferrying tanks and other AFVs over water, which often proved critical in the opening stages of a bridgehead battle.

Soviet logistics for both the 1st and 2nd Ukrainian Fronts were constrained at the start of the March offensive, since Zhukov was unwilling to wait for a real operational pause. Consequently, logistic reserves were slim and Zhukov's tank armies started the offensive with just a two-day reserve of fuel (*boekomplekt*) in hand, which might be stretched to four to five days.[2] Ammunition was also in relatively short supply, with three basic loads (*zapravki*) held by the tank armies. Rybalko's 3GTA calculated that one *boekomplekt* of fuel amounted to 1,400 tons, while one *zapravki* of ammunition was 404 tons. However, in practice, the 3GTA found that it could operate with a minimum of just 86 tons of fuel and 20 tons of ammunition per day, but this meant not all subunits in the formation could advance or fight. Once operations began, Soviet rear area services were expected to push enough ammunition and fuel forward to keep the vanguard units moving.

For this purpose, each tank army had three motor transport battalions (OATb) with a total authorized capacity of about 490 tons, plus additional transport companies at the corps level, but only about 65 per cent of the trucks were operational, reducing capacity to roughly 315 tons. Once weather, terrain, losses and distance to the nearest railhead were factored in, Soviet quartermasters had great difficulty meeting even basic minimum requirements to keep the vanguard moving. The situation was much worse in the infantry armies, like the 60th Army, which had fewer trucks and still employed horse-drawn transport. Given the difficulty in moving basic supplies of fuel and ammunition to the front, Soviet combat troops were expected to live off the land and capture enemy supplies as much as possible to reduce the supply burden.

Air support

General-polkovnik Sergei A. Krasovskiy's 2nd Air Army (2VA) supported Zhukov's 1st Ukrainian Front, while General-leytenant Sergei K. Goriunov's 5th Air Army (5VA) supported Konev's 2nd Ukrainian Front. The 2VA had five bomber regiments equipped with Pe-2s, 14 ground attack regiments equipped with Il-2 Sturmoviks and 15 fighter regiments equipped with a mix of La-5 and Yak fighters; altogether a total of over 800 aircraft, of which about half were operational. Likewise, the 5VA had around 800 aircraft, mostly ground attack and fighters, although only part of this formation was focused against the 1. Panzerarmee sector. Furthermore, most of the Soviet front-line aviation units were stretched to breaking point by March 1944 due to inadequate logistic support and exhausted aircrews. The shortage of trained pilots, after the heavy losses of the previous six months of combat, was particularly acute and forced the Soviet Air Force (VVS) to temporarily sideline many units in order to train the influx of newly minted pilots. As a result, neither the 2VA nor the 5VA was able to commit anything like its full strength to support Zhukov's impending offensive. Overcast weather conditions also hindered Soviet air support, limiting its ability to influence the ground battle.

---

2   Unlike the German VS method, which listed a certain amount of fuel for every vehicle in a formation to move 100km, the Soviet method did not incorporate distance or every vehicle in a given formation. The *boekomplekt* was closer to a basic load of fuel, which could be spent at a rate determined by the commander.

ORDERS OF BATTLE
GERMAN

1. Panzerarmee (Generaloberst Hans-Valentin Hube)

III Panzerkorps (General der Panzertruppen Hermann Breith)
1. Panzer-Division (Generalleutnant Werner Marcks) [Pz IV, 23x Pz V]
16. Panzer-Division (Generalmajor Hans-Ulrich Back) [Pz IV, 3x Pz V]
17. Panzer-Division (Generalleutnant Karl-Friedrich von der Meden) [Pz IV]
II./Panzer-Regiment 23 [23x Panther]
Sturmgeschütz-Brigade 249

LIX Armeekorps (General der Infanterie Kurt von der Chevallerie)
6. Panzer-Division (Generalleutnant Walter Denkert)[3] [23x Pz IV]
schwere Panzerabteilung 509 [28x Tiger]
19. Panzer-Division (Generalleutnant Hans Källner)
SS-Panzerkampfgruppe *Das Reich* (SS-Brigadeführer Heinz Lammerding)
    Panzergruppe Endemann [11x Pz IV, 4x Panther, 3x Tiger, 8x StuG III]; two Panzergrenadier battalions, one artillery battalion
6. SS-Freiwilligen-Sturmbrigade *Langemarck* [6x StuG III]
96. Infanterie-Division (Generalleutnant Richard Wirtz)
291. Infanterie-Division (Generalmajor Oskar Eckholt)
Sturmgeschütz-Brigade 276 [12x StuG] and Sturmgeschütz-Brigade 280 [10x StuG]
schwere Panzerjäger-Abteilung 88 (Major Eberhard Zahn) [42x Hornisse]
Heeresartillerie: 3 towed battalions (1x l.FH18/RSO, 1x 10cm, 1x 15cm), 1 self-propelled battalion (Hummel) and 1 battery (17cm)

XXIV Panzerkorps (General der Panzertruppen Walther Nehring)
20. Panzergrenadier-Division (General der Panzertruppen Georg Jauer)
    Panzer-Abteilung 8 [est. 42x StuG-III], Panzerjäger-Abteilung 20 [Marder II/III]
Kampfgruppe 25. Panzer-Division (Generalleutnant Hans Tröger)
168. Infanterie-Division (Generalleutnant Werner Schmidt-Hammer)
208. Infanterie-Division (Generalleutnant Heinz Piekenbrock)
371. Infanterie-Division (General der Infanterie Hermann Niehoff)
schwere Panzerjäger-Abteilung 731 (sfl.) [Marder II]
Heeresartillerie: 2x towed battalions (1x l.FH/RSO, 1x 21cm Mörser) and 2 batteries (17cm)

XXXXVI Panzerkorps (General der Infanterie Hans Gollnick)[4]
1. Infanterie-Division (Generalleutnant Ernst-Anton von Krosigk)
101. Jäger-Division (General der Gebirgstruppen Emil Vogel)
254. Infanterie-Division (Generalleutnant Alfred Thielmann)
18. Artillerie-Division (Generalleutnant Karl Thoholte) [6x StuG III]
Sturmgeschütz-Brigade 300 [StuG III]

Attached 1. Panzerarmee
Kampfgruppe 11. Panzer-Division [4x Pz III, 14x Pz V]; I./Pz.Regt. 15; Pz.Gren.Regt. 110; Pz.Pi. Btl. 209.
Flak-Regiment 17 [Luftwaffe]

4. Panzerarmee (Generaloberst Erhard Raus) – RIGHT FLANK FORCES ONLY

XXXXVIII Panzerkorps (General der Panzertruppen Hermann Balck)
7. Panzer-Division (Oberst Karl Mauss) [3x Pz V]
    schwere Panzerabteilung 503 [13 operational Tiger] (Hauptmann Scherf)
1. SS-Panzer-Division *Leibstandarte SS Adolf Hitler (LSSAH)* [11x

Panther, 6 Tiger, 2x StuG III] (SS-Brigadeführer Theodore Wisch)[5]
68. Infanterie-Division (Generalmajor Paul Scheuerpflug)

8. Armee (General der Infanterie Otto Wöhler) – LEFT FLANK FORCES ONLY

VII Armeekorps (General der Artillerie Ernst-Eberhard Hell)
34. Infanterie-Division (Generalleutnant Friedrich Hochbaum)
75. Infanterie-Division (Generalleutnant Helmuth Beukemann)
82. Infanterie-Division (Generalleutnant Hans-Walter Heyne)
198. Infanterie-Division (Generalleutnant Hans-Joachim von Horn)
4. Gebirgs-Division (Generalleutnant Julius Braun)
Sturmgeschütz-Brigade 202 and Sturmgeschütz-Brigade 261
Heeresartillerie: 3x towed battalions (1x 10cm, 1x 15cm and 1x 21cm Mörser)

Luftwaffe

Luftflotte 4 (Generaloberst Otto Dessloch)
VIII Fliegerkorps (Generalleutnant Hans Seidemann)
Operating from Lvov-Sknilow, Proskurov, Krosno, Rzeszow, Uman and Kaments-Podolsk airfields
    III./JG 52 [38x Bf 109G]
    Stab, I., II., III./SG 77 [90x Ju 87D, 17x Fw 190F-3, 6x Fw 190G]
    Stab IV., 10.(Pz)/SG 9 [22x Hs 129B]
    Stab, I., II., 14.(Eis)/KG 27 [62x He 111H]
    2.(F)/Aufkl. Grp. 100 [12x Ju-188F], 2.(F)/Aufkl. Grp. 11 [11x Ju 88D]
Transportstaffel VIII Fliegerkorps (Generalmajor Fritz Morzik)
    Lufttransportchef
    I.,IV./Transport-Geschwader 1 (TG 1) [Ju 52]
    I./Transport-Geschwader 3 (TG 3) [Ju 52]
    I./Transport-Geschwader 4 (TG 4) [Ju 52]
    Transportgruppe 30 (TGr.30) [He 111]
    I./KG 4 [26x He 111H]
    Schleppgruppe 2 [He 111, DFS 230 gliders]

Axis Reinforcements

20 March 1944
Hungarian VII Army Corps (Major General István Kiss)
    18th, 19th and 201st Reserve Divisions

23 March 1944
schwere Panzer-Abteilung 507 [45x Tiger]

1–5 April 1944:
II SS-Panzerkorps (SS-Obergruppenführer Paul Hausser)
9. SS-Panzer-Division *Hohenstaufen* (SS-Obergruppenführer Willi Bittrich) [49x Pz IV, 44 StuG]
10. SS Panzer-Division *Frundsberg* (SS-Gruppenführer Karl Fischer von Treuenfeld) [49x Pz IV, 44 StuG]
100. Jäger-Division (Generalleutnant Willibald Utz)
    schwere Panzer-Abteilung 506 [45x Tiger]
367. Infanterie-Division (Generalmajor Georg Zwade)

6 April 1944
schwere Panzerjager-Abteilung 653 [28x Ferdinand tank destroyers]

SOVIET

1st Ukrainian Front (Marshal Georgi K. Zhukov)

1st Tank Army (General-leytenant Mikhail Katukov) [239x tanks]
8th Guards Mechanized Corps (General-major Ivan F. Dremov)
11th Guards Tank Corps (General-leytenant Andrei L. Getman)
64th Guards Tank Brigade (Podpolkovnik Ivan F. Boyko)

---

3   Replaced by Generalmajor Rudolf von Waldenfels on 28 March 1944.
4   Replaced by General der Infanterie Friedrich Schulz on 22 March 1944.

5   On 31 March, Wisch was flown out of the pocket after being wounded and he was replaced by Obersturmbannführer Albert Frey.

3rd Guards Tank Army (General-polkovnik Pavel S. Rybalko) [276x tanks]
9th Mechanized Corps (General-major Konstantin A. Malygin) [32x tanks]
6th Guards Tank Corps (General-major Aleksei P. Panfilov) [166x tanks]
7th Guards Tank Corps (General-major Sergei A. Ivanov) [78x tanks]
4x self-propelled artillery regiments [25x Su-76M]

4th Tank Army (General-leytenant Vasily M. Badanov)[6] [246x tanks]
6th Guards Mechanized Corps (General-leytenant Aleksandr I. Akimov)
10th Guards Tank Corps (General-leytenant Georgi S. Rodin)[7]
2x self-propelled artillery regiments [15x Su-76M]

1st Guards Army (General-polkovnik Andrei A. Grechko)
17th Guards Rifle Corps (68th Guards, 147th, 309th Rifle Divisions)
30th Rifle Corps (121st, 141st Rifle Divisions)
94th Rifle Corps (30th, 99th Rifle Divisions)
107th Rifle Corps (127th, 304th Rifle Divisions)
3rd and 17th Artillery Divisions
93rd Tank Brigade [25x tanks]
4x Guards Heavy Tank Regiments (1st, 12th, 29th, 58th) [80x IS-1, KV-85]
374th Guards Heavy Self-Propelled Artillery Regiment [16x ISU-152]

13th Army (General-leytenant Nikolay P. Pukhov)
24th Rifle Corps (149th, 287th Rifle Divisions)
27th Rifle Corps (6th Guards, 112th, 172nd Rifle Divisions)
76th Rifle Corps (121st Guards, 181st Rifle Divisions)
106th and 162nd Rifle Divisions
1st Guards Cavalry Corps (1st, 2nd, 7th Guards Cavalry Divisions)
6th Guards Cavalry Corps (8th Guards, 13th Guards, 8th Cavalry Divisions)

18th Army (General-leytenant Evgeniy P. Zhuravlev)
11th Rifle Corps (271st, 276th, 316th Rifle Divisions)
22nd Rifle Corps (129th Guards, 71st, 317th, 395th Rifle Divisions)
52nd Rifle Corps (117th Guards, 24th, 161st Rifle Divisions)

38th Army (General-polkovnik Kirill S. Moskalenko)
67th Rifle Corps (151st, 221st Rifle Divisions)
74th Rifle Corps (183rd, 237th, 305th Rifle Divisions)
101st Rifle Corps (70th Guards, 211th, 241st Rifle Divisions)
106th Rifle Corps (100th, 135th, 155th Rifle Divisions)
39th Separate Tank Regiment [20x T-34/76]
3x self-propelled artillery regiments [20x Su-76M]

60th Army (General-polkovnik Ivan D. Cherniakhovsky)
4th Guards Tank Corps (General-major Pavel P. Poluboyarov)
18th Guards Rifle Corps (148th, 280th Rifle Divisions)
15th Rifle Corps (322nd, 336th Rifle Divisions)
23rd Rifle Corps (8th, 226th, 351st Rifle Divisions)
28th Rifle Corps (140th, 246th Rifle Divisions)
1st Guards Artillery Division
59th Separate Tank Regiment [20x T-34/76]
2x self-propelled artillery regiments [15x Su-76M]

2nd Air Army [2VA] (General-polkovnik Sergei A. Krasovskiy)
4th Bomber Aviation Corps [4BAK]
    202nd Bomber Aviation Division [202 BAD]: 36 GBAP, 18 BAP, 797 BAP [Pe-2]
    219th Bomber Aviation Division [219 BAD]: 6, 38 BAP [Pe-2]
5th Ground Attack Aviation Corps [5 ShaK]
    4th Guards Ground Attack Aviation Division [4 GShaD]: 90, 91, 92 GdShaP [Il-2]

    264th Ground Attack Aviation Division [264 ShaD]: 235, 451, 809 ShaP [Il-2]
    331st Fighter Aviation Division [331 IAD]: 122, 179, 513 IAP [Yak-1/Yak-7b/Yak-9]
5th Fighter Aviation Corps [5 IAK]
    8th Guards Fighter Aviation Division [8 GIAD]: 40, 41, 88 GIAP [La-5]
    256th Fighter Aviation Division [256 IAD]: 32, 91, 728 IAP [Yak-1/Yak-9]
10th Fighter Aviation Corps [10 IAK]
    10th Guards Fighter Aviation Division [10 GIAD]: 111, 113 GIAP [La-5], 112 GIAP [Yak-1]
    235th Fighter Aviation Division [235 IAD]: 3 GIAP, 180, 181 IAP [La-5]
10th Guards Ground Attack Aviation Division [10 GShaD]: 165, 166, 167 GShaP [Il-2]
224th Ground Attack Aviation Division [224 ShaD]: 565, 571, 996 ShaP and 227th Ground Attack Aviation Division [227 ShaD]: 525, 637 ShaP [Il-2]

2nd Ukrainian Front (Marshal Ivan S. Konev)

2nd Tank Army (General-leytenant Semyon I. Bogdanov) [175 tanks, 65 assault guns][8]
3rd Tank Corps (General-major Nikolai M. Telyakov)
16th Tank Corps (General-major Ivan V. Dubovoy)
11th Guards Tank Brigade
8, 13th Guards Separate Tank Regiments [total of 32x IS-2]
136th Rifle Division

6th Tank Army (General-leytenant Andrei G. Kravchenko)
5th Mechanized Corps (General-leytenant Mikhail V. Volkov)
5th Guards Tank Corps (General-leytenant Vasily M. Alekseev)
156th Guards Separate Tank Regiment

40th Army (General-leytenant Filipp F. Zhmachenko)
50th Rifle Corps (4th Guards Airborne Division, 240th Rifle Division)
51st Rifle Corps (42nd Guards, 133rd, 232nd Rifle Divisions)
104th Rifle Corps (38th, 74th, 163rd Rifle Divisions)
1st Rifle Brigade (Czech)

5th Air Army [5VA] (General-leytenant Sergei K. Goriunov)
2nd Guards Bomber Aviation Corps [2 GBAK]
    1st Guards Bomber Aviation Division [1 GBAD]: 80, 81, 82 GBAP [Pe-2]
    8th Guards Bomber Aviation Division [8 GBAD]: 160, 161, 162 GBAP [Pe-2]
1st Guards Ground Attack Aviation Corps [1 GShaK]
    8th Guards Ground Attack Aviation Division [8 GShaD]: 140, 142, 143 GShaP [Il-2]
    9th Guards Ground Attack Aviation Division [9 GShaD]: 141, 144, 155 GShaP [Il-2]
    12th Guards Ground Attack Aviation Division [12 GShaD]: 187, 188, 190 GShaP [Il-2] 8th Guards Ground Attack Aviation Division [8 GShaD]
6th Ground Attack Aviation Corps [6 ShaK]
    197th Ground Attack Aviation Division [197 ShaD]: 618, 765, 805 ShaP [Il-2]
    198th Ground Attack Aviation Division [198 ShaD]: 41, 567, 945 ShaP [Il-2]
4th Fighter Aviation Corps [4 IAK]
    294th Fighter Aviation Division [294 IAD]: 6, 183, 427 IAP [Yak-1/Yak-7b]
    302nd Fighter Aviation Division [302 IAD]: 193, 240, 297 IAP [La-5]
7th Fighter Aviation Corps [7 IAK]
    205th Fighter Aviation Division [205 IAD]: 27, 438, 508 IAP [P-39]
    304th Fighter Aviation Division [304 IAD]: 21, 69, 211 GIAP [P-39]

---

6   Badanov was seriously wounded on 29 March and replaced by General-leytenant Dmitri D. Leliushenko.

7   Rodin was relieved of command on 15 March 1944 and replaced by General-major Evtikhiy E. Belov.

8   On 3 March, 2 TA had 124 T-34, 19 Valentine and 32 IS-2 tanks, plus 43 Su-76, 16x Su-85 and 6 Su-152.

THE CAMPAIGN

THE FIRST PHASE OF ZHUKOV'S OFFENSIVE, 4–20 MARCH 1944

Despite being critically short of manpower and resources, von Manstein authorized his subordinate army commanders to conduct an active defence, striking at the enemy to disrupt their preparations for an offensive. On 2 March, SS-Kampfgruppe *Das Reich*, supported by 30 Ju 87 Stukas, launched a spoiling attack near Zhemelyntsi (12km east of Yampil) against the forward positions of the 60th Army. However, the Soviets were ready and repulsed the attack, destroying two Tigers and three Panthers. The lead elements of Generalleutnant Walter Denkert's 6. Panzer-Division had just arrived in the Belgorodka sector but were not yet fully ready for combat. The 6. SS-Freiwilligen-Sturmbrigade *Langemarck* (comprising 2,000 Flemish volunteers) held the strongpoint in Yampil with an infantry battalion and six Stug III assault guns, while the remainder of its troops were spread out in screening positions to the east of the town. In point of fact, the Germans had no real HKL between Yampil and Shepetovka, nor even firm contact between Hube's and Raus' adjoining armies. Balck's XXXXVIII Panzerkorps and von der Chevallerie's LIX Armeekorps, both responsible for the inter-army boundary zone, were not even fully aware of each other's positions.

At 0615hrs on 4 March, just before dawn, Cherniakhovsky's 60th Army began a 90-minute artillery preparation with over 240 guns against the sector between Yampil and Belgorodka. However, it was an overcast morning, with heavy fog, which hindered artillery observation. Nor did the dispersed German strongpoints offer very good targets. With morning temperature just above freezing (2°C or 35°F), a thaw was setting in and vehicle mobility was impaired by partly frozen mud. When the bombardment lifted around 0745hrs, shock groups from the 15th and 23rd Rifle Corps began advancing toward their initial objectives. German observers reported great masses of Soviet infantry advancing across the snow-flecked plain, along with small numbers of

A Tiger tank camouflaged alongside a hut in a Ukrainian village. The Germans tried to conceal their tanks prior to the Soviet offensives, but it also proved more difficult to mobilize dispersed tanks to mount an effective counterattack when needed. (Fotoarchiv für Zeitgeschichte/Archiv/Süddeutsche Zeitung Photo)

The first phase of Zhukov's offensive, 4–20 March 1944

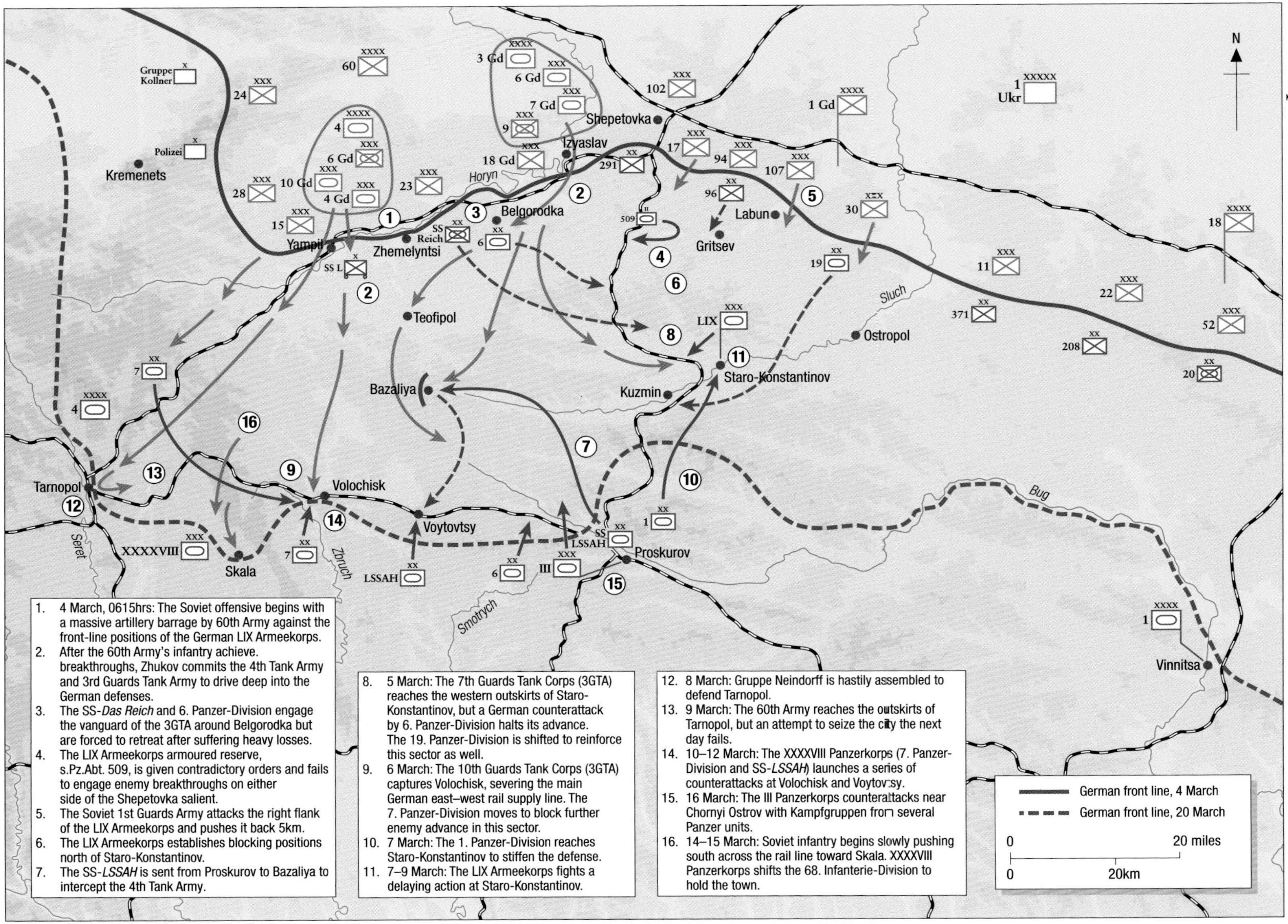

N

Legend:
- ▬▬▬ German front line, 4 March
- ▬ ▬ German front line, 20 March

0 — 20 miles
0 — 20km

Map labels (units and places):

18, 52, 20, 1, Vinnitsa, 1 Ukr, 22, 208, 30, Ostropol, 11, 371, 19, 1 Gd, 5, 107, 94, 96, Labun, Gritsev, Staro-Konstantinov, LIX, 11, 10, 1, Proskurov, 17, 102, Shepetovka, 291, Izyaslav, 509, 4, 6, 8, Kuzmin, 7, SS LSSAH, 15, III, 6, 7 Gd, 6 Gd, 9, 18 Gd, 3 Gd, Belgorodka, 6, 2, Teofipol, Bazaliya, Voytovtsy, LSSAH, 60, 23, SS Reich, Zhemelyntsi, 1, 2, 9, Volochisk, 14, 7, Zbruch, 4, 6 Gd, 4 Gd, Yampil, SS L, 16, Skala, 13, 24, 10 Gd, 28, 15, 7, 4, XXXXVIII, Kremenets, Gruppe Kollner, Polizei, 12, Tarnopol, Seret, Bug, Sluch, Horyn, Smotrych

Numbered annotations:

1. 4 March, 0615hrs: The Soviet offensive begins with a massive artillery barrage by 60th Army against the front-line positions of the German LIX Armeekorps. After the 60th Army's infantry achieve breakthroughs, Zhukov commits the 4th Tank Army and 3rd Guards Tank Army to drive deep into the German defenses.

2. The SS-*Das Reich* and 6. Panzer-Division engage the vanguard of the 3GTA around Belgorodka but are forced to retreat after suffering heavy losses.

3. The LIX Armeekorps armoured reserve, s.Pz.Abt. 509, is given contradictory orders and fails to engage enemy breakthroughs on either side of the Shepetovka salient.

4. The Soviet 1st Guards Army attacks the right flank of the LIX Armeekorps and pushes it back 5km.

5. The LIX Armeekorps establishes blocking positions north of Staro-Konstantinov.

6. The SS-*LSSAH* is sent from Proskurov to Bazaliya to intercept the 4th Tank Army.

7.

8. 5 March: The 7th Guards Tank Corps (3GTA) reaches the western outskirts of Staro-Konstantinov, but a German counterattack by 6. Panzer-Division halts its advance. The 19. Panzer-Division is shifted to reinforce this sector as well.

9. 6 March: The 10th Guards Tank Corps (3GTA) captures Volochisk, severing the main German east–west rail supply line. The 7. Panzer-Division moves to block further enemy advance in this sector.

10. 7 March: The 1. Panzer-Division reaches Staro-Konstantinov to stiffen the defense.

11. 7–9 March: The LIX Armeekorps fights a delaying action at Staro-Konstantinov.

12. 8 March: Gruppe Neindorff is hastily assembled to defend Tarnopol.

13. 9 March: The 60th Army reaches the outskirts of Tarnopol, but an attempt to seize the city the next day fails.

14. 10–12 March: The XXXXVIII Panzerkorps (7. Panzer-Division and SS-*LSSAH*) launches a series of counterattacks at Volochisk and Voytovtsy.

15. 16 March: The III Panzerkorps counterattacks near Chornyi Ostrov with Kampfgruppen from several Panzer units.

16. 14–15 March: Soviet infantry begins slowly pushing south across the rail line toward Skala. XXXXVIII Panzerkorps shifts the 68. Infanterie-Division to hold the town.

close support tanks, but little artillery support was available to break up the enemy formations. Nor was the Luftwaffe able to intervene due to overcast skies with low cloud cover. The SS-*Langemarck* had no chance of holding against this onslaught, and the battalion holding the fortified position in Yampil was attacked from all sides and quickly overrun. Without further ado, the survivors hastily retreated to the south-east, enlarging the already wide gap in the German front. By 1300hrs, Cherniakhovsky's shock groups had occupied Yampil, and Zhukov decided to commit Badanov's 4th Tank Army (4TA) into the breach. Since the 18th Rifle Corps had seized crossings over the Horyn River, Zhukov also committed Rybalko's 3rd Guards Tank Army (3GTA) to advance upon Belgorodka.

General der Infanterie Kurt von der Chevallerie, commander of the LIX Armeekorps, had deployed the SS-Panzerkampfgruppe *Das Reich* (with three Tigers and 11 PzKpfw IV tanks) near Zhemelyntsi, while a large Kampfgruppe from the 6. Panzer-Division (with 23 PzKpfw IV tanks) was deployed in and around the town of Belgorodka. These two German armoured battlegroups were essentially ordered to conduct a zone defence along the Yampil–Belgorodka road, without benefit of significant support units. Off to the west, Badanov's 4TA plunged through the penetration corridor centred on Yampil and easily brushed aside the small blocking detachments that Balck's XXXXVIII Panzerkorps had established in this sector. In the four hours prior to sunset at 1756hrs, Badanov's tanks were able to advance up to 15km and reach all their first-day objectives. On Badanov's right flank, the Soviet 13th Army also attacked and pushed back the German screening forces near Kremenets, thereby widening the tear in von Manstein's front to about 30km in width. Only Rybalko's tankers faced any serious opposition on the first day, when the three Tigers from the SS-*Das Reich* Kampfgruppe shot up some of their lead T-34s. However, the 6th Guards Tank Corps flowed around the open flanks of the small German Kampfgruppe, surrounding it. In desperation, the SS-*Das Reich* tanks tried to escape via the town of Zhemelyntsi, which they discovered was already enemy-occupied. One Tiger was lost in a swamp and the other two were knocked out by massed Soviet tank and anti-tank fire, while nine of 11 PzKpfw IV tanks were also lost. Although the SS-*Das Reich* claimed to have knocked out 31 Soviet tanks, it had lost a good portion of its armour in the brief action. The Kampfgruppe from 6. Panzer-Division fought a brisk delaying action against the 7th Guards Tank Corps (7GTC) north of Belgorodka, destroying at least 11 T-34s, at a cost of 13 PzKpfw IV tanks. However, two Soviet rifle divisions began a pincer attack on the German Panzergrenadiers holding Belgorodka, supported by the tanks of 7GTC. The 6. Panzer-Division held as long as possible, but finally was forced to break contact and retreat southward toward Staro-Konstantinov. Only four German tanks from 6. Panzer-Division were still operational by the end of the first day of the Soviet offensive and they had exhausted their ammunition.

General-polkovnik Andrei A. Grechko's 1st Guards Army also attacked on the morning of 4 March, with its main effort made in the Labun sector east of the town of Shepetovka. The town of Shepetovka itself had been captured by the Red Army in early February, but the German 291. Infanterie-Division was holding positions just south of the city, with the 96. Infanterie-Division and 19. Panzer-Division covering its right flank. The schwere Panzerabteilung 509 was deployed in tactical reserve with 28 Tiger tanks. Grechko relied

A PzKpfw IV tank burns in the snow. The 1. Panzerarmee started the Kamenets-Podolsky campaign with about 100 PzKpfw IV tanks, mostly the Ausf H model. In the opening days of Zhukov's offensive, the Germans lost many of their tanks involved in the covering force battles. (From the fonds of the RGAKFD in Krasnogorsk via Stavka)

upon his massed artillery and infantry to achieve a breakthrough in the sector held by the 96. Infanterie-Division, but he had limited armour to exploit the breach. The LIX Armeekorps responded to this breakthrough by sending the s.Pz.Abt. 509 eastward to counterattack Grechko's lead elements, but then someone decided that the situation in the 6. Panzer-Division sector was more dangerous and ordered the battalion to reverse course and proceed to the west; consequently, the Tiger battalion held in tactical reserve failed to contain either of the enemy attacks. The 19. Panzer-Division was actually holding a 15km stretch of front line, which proved far too much for its four Panzergrenadier-Bataillone and limited number of tanks. Soviet infantry from the 30th Rifle Corps simply pushed through the gaps in the German HKL, enveloping Panzergrenadier-Regiment 73 and forcing the entire division to fall back nearly 5km. By the end of the first day of his offensive, Zhukov had pushed back both flanks of von der Chevallerie's LIX Armeekorps and opened a large gap between the 1. Panzerarmee and 4. Panzerarmee, through which two tank armies were pouring.

Von der Chevallerie, in his headquarters in Staro-Konstantinov, was uncertain about the chaotic situation at the front and he began issuing conflicting orders on the evening of 4/5 March. He authorized the SS-*Das Reich* and 6. Panzer-Division to withdraw toward the Sluch River (which they were already doing) but ordered the 291. Infanterie-Division to form a blocking position on the Shepetovka–Staro-Konstantinov road. Major Eberhard Zahn's schwere Panzerjäger-Abteilung 88, which had just arrived by rail in Staro-Konstantinov, was ordered to send a detachment of seven Hornisse tank destroyers to support the infantry. Zahn quickly discovered that the infantry were in full retreat and that the 19. Panzer-Division (which had lost its few remaining operational tanks) was also falling back under pressure. Zahn's tank destroyers managed to destroy some T-34s in a short action near dusk but were left without infantry support and obliged to fall back, as well. Von der Chevallerie also requested that Breith commit the 1. Panzer-Division from III Panzerkorps to the Staro-Konstantinov sector to help stem the Soviet breakthrough; the division began moving north in piecemeal fashion during the night, hindered by muddy roads. Although the LIX Armeekorps claimed to have destroyed over 125 Soviet AFVs on the first day of Zhukov's offensive, nowhere had the Germans managed to stop the enemy shock groups.

Von Manstein was unhappy with von der Chevallerie's slapdash responses and tried to direct the limited reserves to where he thought they might do the most good. In particular, he assigned SS-Brigadeführer Theodor Wisch's SS-*LSSAH* to Balck's XXXXVIII Panzerkorps and ordered it to move 50km from Proskurov to Bazaliya (32km south-east of Yampil) to try and intercept Badanov's 4th Tank Army before it drove a deeper wedge between the 4 PzAOK and 1 PzAOK. Von Manstein trusted Balck to fight a clever mobile delaying action with meagre forces, as he had already demonstrated in the Battle of the Chir River in December 1942. Balck shifted Oberst Karl Mauss' 7. Panzer-

Division to the west of Bazaliya to assist the SS-*LSSAH*. Yet no sooner had the first SS-Panzergrenadiers reached Bazaliya than they were in contact with the lead elements of the 6th Guards Tank Corps from Rybalko's 3GTA. Now von Manstein realized that two Soviet tank armies were pushing into the gap, not one. The SS-*LSSAH* managed to form hasty blocking positions in a ring around Bazaliya but quickly discovered that Soviet armour was slipping around both their flanks. Badanov's and Rybalko's tankers had

The Hornisse (Hornet) tank destroyer combined an 8.8cm Pak 43 gun atop the modified chassis of a PzKpfw IV tank, which resulted in a powerful mobile anti-tank system. The schwere Panzerjäger-Abteilung 88, equipped with 42 Hornisse, reached Hube's army just as Zhukov's offensive was about to begin. (Author)

a good day, in that losses were fairly light and all the initial objectives were reached. While Soviet infantry cleared the towns and villages, the Soviet armour continued to press forward during the night of 4/5 March, spreading panic among German support units. Zhukov was surprised that the German front line had collapsed so quickly across such a wide sector and urged his army-level commanders to accelerate their attacks.

By the morning of 5 March, Wisch's SS-*LSSAH* was nearly encircled by Rybalko's tankers at Bazaliya, while the vanguard of Generalmajor Sergei A. Ivanov's 7th Guards Tank Corps (7GTC) was approaching the western outskirts of Staro-Konstantinov. Meanwhile, the bulk of the LIX Armeekorps combat units (including SS-*Das Reich* and 1. Panzer-Division) were in tenuous positions north of Staro-Konstantinov, with the Soviets threatening to cut them off, as well. The battered Kampfgruppe from 6. Panzer-Division had fallen back into Staro-Konstantinov – it had limited remaining combat capability. During the hasty retreat, the Germans had been forced to abandon a considerable amount of supplies, broken-down vehicles and artillery pieces that lacked prime movers.

Retreating in the dark, along frozen, muddy roads, also proved difficult and added to the general confusion. Von der Chevallerie had few tactical options since Hitler had already ordered that Staro-Konstantinov would be held at all costs, even if encircled. Consequently, von der Chevallerie opted to conduct local counterattacks to try and prevent the enemy pincers from closing around the LIX Armeekorps, while hoping for the enemy offensive to abate. He ordered Oberstleutnant Franz Bäke, one of the star players in the Korsun Pocket relief operation, to lead a counterattack with some Tigers from s.Pz.Abt. 509 and elements of the 6. Panzer-Division in an effort to push the Soviets back from the western suburbs. Bäke claimed to have knocked out 17 Soviet tanks for the loss of two Tigers, but the dangerous situation was unchanged. The LIX Armeekorps was not tied in with friendly forces on either flank, and its supply lines to Proskurov were tenuous. At points, the German weakness in the field was almost comical, as when three Tiger tanks were assigned to help a Bäckerei-Kompanie (Bakery Company) hold a key village. Von der Chevallerie decided to shift the 19. Panzer-Division to the south-west of the city to protect his escape route, while assigning the 1. Panzer-Division to guard the northern approaches. Nevertheless, Wisch's SS-*LSSAH* was forced to evacuate its blocking position at Bazaliya and retreat southward to the Bug River.

A Soviet T-34 with a mounted squad of *Desantniki* infantry passes a burning Tiger in early 1944. During the initial phase of Zhukov's offensive in March, the Tiger tank-equipped units suffered significant losses because they often had very little friendly infantry or artillery in support. (From the fonds of the RGAKFD in Krasnogorsk via Stavka)

Hube's problems continued to grow on 5 March, as Zhuravlev's 18th Army launched its attack in the XXIV Panzerkorps sector north of Vinnitsa, while Moskalenko's 38th Army attacked the XXXXVI Panzerkorps to the east. Hube had very little armour protecting his right flank and his weakened infantry divisions could not stop the Soviets from achieving breakthroughs in both sectors. Zhukov then committed part of Katukov's 1st Tank Army behind the 38th Army, pushing boldly toward Vinnitsa. Even worse, Konev's 2nd Ukrainian Front began its own offensive against Wöhler's 8. Armee on the same day, with the 27th Army massing six rifle divisions against a single infantry division from the VII Armeekorps. The 198. Infanterie-Division was quickly crushed, then Konev committed Kravchenko's 6th Tank Army into the breach. The German VII Armeekorps was torn apart, with four divisions (34., 75., 82. and 198.) retreating west toward Hube's 1. Panzerarmee, while the other division (4. Gebirgs) retreated east toward Wöhler's 8. Armee. The 16. Panzer-Division also retreated into the 1. PzAOK zone. In two days, Konev's forces advanced 20km and created an irreparable breach between 1. PzAOK and the 8. Armee. Von Manstein had no significant reserves to commit, and the Luftwaffe was powerless to stem multiple breakthroughs, leaving Hube's army in a near hopeless operational position.

Zhukov continued to press his advantage on 6 March, with Badanov's 4TA surging forward to capture Volochisk with General-leytenant Georgi S. Rodin's 10th Guards Tank Corps (10GTC), thereby severing the main German rail line between Tarnopol and Proskurov. Balck's XXXXVIII Panzerkorps, guarding the right flank of Raus' 4. PzAOK, was also obliged to defend the city of Tarnow, which Hitler had designated as a fortress (*fester Platz*) with Führer Order No. 11 on 8 March. Consequently, Balck formed a 4,500-man Kampfgruppe under Generalmajor Egon von Neindorff (reinforced with one Tiger, a battery of six 'Grille' self-propelled 15cm infantry guns and some Marder II tank destroyers) to hold Tarnopol. Von Neindorff found that the city had no anti-tank ditches, mines nor other obstacles to delay the enemy advance. Before the German garrison even had a chance to begin creating defensive positions, the lead elements of Generalmajor Pavel P. Poluboyarov's 4th Guards Tank Corps (4GTC) and one rifle division reached the outskirts of the city on 9 March. The next day, the Soviets mounted a hasty attack to try and storm Tarnopol, but the defence managed to hold.

Meanwhile, Balck also had to make an effort to try and plug the 50km-wide gap between 4. PzAOK and 1. PzAOK before the Soviet tank armies drove a deeper wedge between the two German armies. On 10 March, Balck ordered Wisch's SS-*LSSAH* and s.Pz.Abt. 503 to attack westward from the Voytovtsy rail station in order to link up with Mauss' 7. Panzer-Division attacking toward the east. Altogether, these depleted units barely had 35 operational tanks and they were being sent to halt the advance of Soviet tank formations that still fielded roughly 300 tanks in this sector. Yet, unknown to the Germans, the Soviet armour had outrun its supplies, and many forward units were virtually out of ammunition and fuel. Leytenant Evgeni Bessonov, a motorized infantry platoon leader in the 6th Guards Mechanized Corps (6GMC/4TA) at Volochisk, later stated that his unit went into action with barely any ammunition (just 20 rounds in his PPSh-41 sub-machine gun and one belt of ammunition for the platoon heavy machine gun). Bessonov also noted that many of the Soviet tanks were already immobilized by minor faults. Logistics were the Achilles heel of the Soviet armoured steamroller, which was grinding to a halt after an advance of barely 70km.

Balck's counterattack began on 11 March, with Mauss' 7. Panzer-Division attacking two corps (6GMC, 10GTC) of Badanov's 4TA at Volochisk, while Wisch's SS-*LSSAH* attacked two corps (9MC, 6GTC) of Rybalko's 3GTA near Voytovtsy. Since the weather had cleared up a bit during the ongoing thaw, the Luftwaffe was able to provide some much-needed close air support. Luftflotte 4 unleashed the Hs 129B ground attack planes from Hauptmann Rudolf-Heinz Ruffer's 10.(Pz)/SG 9, which shot up some of Badanov's tanks. A series of skirmishes continued along the rail line from Voytovtsy to Volochisk over the next several days, with both sides sustaining heavy losses. The Stavka was so alarmed by this sudden display of German Panzer strength that it ordered Zhukov to shift his entire front to the defensive and focus on replenishing his forward units before resuming his own offensive. Wisch's SS-*LSSAH* claimed to have eliminated about 40 enemy AFVs with its counterattack but its own combat strength was reduced to just 1,239 troops, six tanks (two Tiger, four Panther), three assault guns and two Wespe self-propelled howitzers. Breith's III Panzerkorps also scraped together about 30 tanks from the 17. and 19. Panzer-Divisionen and s.Pz.Abt. 509 (12 Tigers) in order to launch a counterattack on 16 March against Rybalko's stalled armour west of Proskurov, near Chornyi Ostrov. Balck received some reinforcements – the 68. and 359. Infanterie-Divisionen – which he used to create a line of sorts between Tarnopol and Skala.

Amazingly, Balck's small armoured counterattacks not only temporarily halted Zhukov's main effort but were even able to achieve the objective of re-establishing a common front between Raus' 4. PzAOK and Hube's 1. PzAOK. Of course, the front was quite porous, but there should have been no connection at all at this point. It was also evident that due to the efforts of Balck and Breith, Zhukov failed to take either of his two intermediate objectives – Tarnopol and Proskurov – in the first round of his offensive. Nor had Zhukov managed to encircle or destroy any German formations, although the survivors of the SS-*Langemarck* Brigade had been rolled into the SS-*Das Reich* Kampfgruppe. Furthermore, Rybalko's 3GTA had suffered significant losses and was no longer fully combat effective. Before he could resume his offensive, Zhukov had to shift Katukov's 1st Tank Army (1TA) west to reinforce his main effort. Zhukov decided he had to blame somebody for this setback and he selected Rodin, commander of the 10GTC,

Two Tigers with infantry support wait for the enemy. The Germans tried to use their armour and limited number of Panzergrenadiers to block the Soviet armoured spearheads, but small teams like this often found themselves encircled if they did not withdraw in a timely manner. (Nik Cornish at www.stavka.photos)

as his scapegoat. Claiming that Rodin had provided inaccurate messages about the position of his tank corps around Volochisk, Zhukov relieved him of command and sent him off to obscurity in a training assignment. As usual, Zhukov had no qualms about displays of personal vindictiveness, *pour encourager les autres*.

While Balck was desperately fighting to close the gap between the two Panzer armies, Hube's 1. PzAOK concentrated on trying to stabilize the front between Proskurov and Vinnitsa (both of which Hitler had designated as *feste Plätze*). Hube tasked von der Chevallerie with fighting a delaying action at Staro-Konstantinov with the LIX Armeekorps in order to hold off Grechko's 1st Guards Army for several days. Thanks to the successful covering force efforts of Generalleutnant Werner Marcks' 1. Panzer-Division, both the 96. and 291. Infanterie-Divisionen succeeded in withdrawing toward Staro-Konstantinov to stiffen the defence. However, Grechko's infantry skirted around the open flanks, threatening to isolate the LIX Armeekorps in Staro-Konstantinov. By the end of 7 March, Hitler decided to allow LIX Armeekorps to pull back to form a tighter perimeter around the city, but did not finally authorize a withdrawal until the next day. Once permission was granted, von der Chevallerie ordered Marcks' 1. Panzer-Division to conduct a rearguard operation to hold the city until the morning of 9 March, while the rest of the LIX Armeekorps withdrew toward Proskurov. Marcks' division was forced to 'run the gauntlet' with Soviet forces closing in from three sides, but succeeded in escaping southward after accomplishing its mission. Shortly thereafter, Grechko's 1st Guards Army occupied the city. Oberst Helmut Bechler, commander of Grenadier-Regiment 504, also conducted a tough rearguard action at the town of Zapadintsy (20km south-west of Staro-Konstantinov), which halted the Soviet pursuit for three vital days while the LIX Armeekorps organized the defence of Proskurov.

Due to the disruption of the main rail line from Tarnopol, the Luftwaffe began flying in a small amount of daily supplies to the 1. Panzerarmee. Beginning on 7 March, 30 He 111 bombers delivered 6.6 tons of petrol to the Proskurov airfield. Two days later, another 15 tons of fuel and artillery ammunition were delivered. On 11 March, Luftflotte 4 began dropping supply cannisters directly to the III Panzerkorps and XXIV Panzerkorps, some loaded with tank ammunition, some with fuel. Nevertheless, the air resupply operation at this point was sporadic and amounted to barely 4 per cent of daily requirements.

When Uman was overrun, the s.Pz.Abt. 503 lost 21 of its Tigers abandoned in the repair facility at Potash, north-east of the city. Once the Ostheer began retreating, it was often forced to abandon more equipment than was actually lost in combat. (Courtesy of the Central Museum of the Armed Forces, Moscow via Stavka)

On Hube's right flank, Konev's 2nd Ukrainian Front continued to widen the breach between 1. PzAOK and the left flank of Wöhler's 8. Armee. Konev committed his 2nd Tank Army (2TA) and 5th Guards Tank Army (5GTA), which smashed through any remaining resistance and headed straight for the Dniester River. By 10 March, Konev's armour was in Uman and the smashed remnants of the 8. Armee were in full retreat to the south-east. Indeed, the German retreat was so precipitous that a major depot at Potash (north-east of Uman) was abandoned virtually intact, enabling Bogdanov's 2TA to capture 390 tons of fuel. Emboldened by Konev's success, Zhukov ordered his two left flank armies – Zhuravlev's 18th Army and Moskalenko's 38th Army – to step up their own attacks against Hube's right flank. Zhuravlev succeeded in piercing General der Panzertruppen Walther Nehring's XXIV Panzerkorps front and reaching Khmel'nik on 10 March, but Moskalenko encountered tough resistance from XXXXVI Panzerkorps and made slower progress. Nevertheless, von Manstein could see the writing on the wall and on 11 March he ordered Hube to pull his right flank formations back behind the Bug River. However, it was too late. Konev's offensive was achieving spectacular results compared to Zhukov's semi-stalled offensive, and Bogdanov's 2TA spearhead crossed the Bug on 13 March. By the afternoon of 17 March, Bogdanov had reached Yampol on the Dniester River, and two days later the 6th Tank Army seized Mogilev-Podolsky. Granted, Bogdanov had only about 30 AFVs across the river, but it was enough. As a result, not only was Hube's right flank completely exposed to envelopment, but 1. PzAOK was also nearly isolated by these enemy advances. With the rail line to Tarnopol already severed by Zhukov's armour, Hube's only remaining line of communications lay southward through Kamenets-Podolsky and Chernovtsy into northern Romania.

Given the onset of these massive Soviet offensives and the threat to Heeresgruppe Süd, Hitler should have been focused on the situation in western Ukraine. Instead, he was distracted by the political situation in Hungary involving Admiral Miklós Horthy's sub rosa attempts to seek a separate peace, and his intransigence in handing over 500,000 Hungarian Jews to the SS for liquidation. Even though the Hungarian situation was not an immediate crisis – unlike what was happening to von Manstein's command – Hitler decided that resolving his Hungarian problems took precedence. Thus, on 19 March, Hitler ordered the Wehrmacht to execute Operation *Margarethe* – the military occupation of Hungary. Over 100,000 German troops, including the full-strength Panzer-Lehr Division, poured into Hungary. Horthy quickly acquiesced to Hitler's demands, although the Wehrmacht was obliged to keep several divisions in Budapest to ensure compliance. Meanwhile, very few reinforcements were going to von Manstein's disintegrating command. Adding insult to injury, after the Hungarian operation concluded, the Panzer-Lehr Division was sent to France and most of the other divisions were dispersed to Italy or the Balkans.

Soviet soldiers inspect an abandoned Panther tank, near Uman, 10 March 1944. Note the PzKpfw IV tank and Hummel self-propelled gun farther back, indicating that this might be the maintenance facility at Potash. Most of the German armour was inoperative at the start of the Soviet offensive, since spare parts were scarce. (Author)

SOVIET SUPPLY COLUMNS STRUGGLE FORWARD THROUGH THE MUD, 15 MARCH 1944 (PP. 42–43)

During the first five days of the 1st Ukrainian Front spring offensive, the vanguard units expended most of their on-hand ammunition and fuel, forcing Zhukov to order a nine-day halt for supply columns to restock his front-line tank armies. As it turned out, the mobility of the Red Army was hindered by the Ukrainian mud just as much as the Wehrmacht's, if not more, due to the lack of tracked logistic vehicles. Each Soviet tank army had three motor transport battalions used to push ammunition and fuel forward from the nearest railhead to distribution points near the front, although the distances involved usually meant one supply run per truck company per day. Here, a column **(1)** of American-built Studebaker US6 cargo trucks is arriving at a field distribution point **(2)** near Volochisk to deliver ammunition and fuel to elements of Badanov's 4th Tank Army. A German Panther tank **(3)**, disabled in a previous rearguard action, lies as mute observer in a nearby field. As the truck convoy arrives, the crew of one T-34/76 Model 1943 **(4)** is already beginning to refuel their tank, transferring fuel from drums via a hand pump, which was a tedious process. The art of tactical refuelling is an essential – but often overlooked – ingredient of armoured operations.

Conducting tactical refuelling at night in order to avoid enemy air raids can be even more challenging, since it was not unusual for supply columns to go astray in the dark.

Logistics was the Achilles heel of the Red Army in 1943–44, but the arrival of over 200,000 Lend-Lease Studebaker trucks helped to partially redress this imbalance. The Studebaker could handle the thick Ukrainian mud, unlike many of the German cargo trucks **(5)** and ensured that Zhukov's spearhead units could continue to receive at least a daily trickle of supplies. While rated as having a cargo capacity of 2.5 tons, the Red Army often increased the loads on the Studebaker up to 4 tons, which reduced mobility on muddy roads. With a standard load, a single Studebaker could deliver enough fuel to refill four T-34/76 tanks; eight trucks could refill a tank battalion. Unlike the Germans, the VVS had minimal ability to deliver supplies to forward units by air, so the tank armies were totally dependent upon their truck battalions to sustain their advances. The fact that the resupply effort took nine days to complete proved to be more of an obstacle to the fulfilment of Zhukov's operational goals than any resistance offered by Hube's 1. Panzerarmee.

One can only ponder what the eight divisions Hitler committed to the Hungarian escapade might have achieved if they had been sent eastward in a timely manner to reinforce 4. Panzerarmee's counterattacks around Tarnopol or to assist the withdrawal of Hube's 1. PzAOK. Certainly, a full-strength unit like the Panzer-Lehr Division could have achieved more than the scarecrow Panzer-Divisionen that Raus and Hube were forced to employ. As it was, the counterattacks by Balck's XXXXVIII Panzerkorps inflicted significant damage upon Rybalko's 3GTA and seriously upset Zhukov's timetable.

A Soviet 82mm mortar crew crossing the Bug River near Vinnitsa, around 18 March 1944. The Red Army's ability to 'bounce' rivers often caught the Germans by surprise. (Author)

In any case, few German reinforcements reached Raus or Hube in their moment of crisis, thereby allowing Zhukov to maintain the operational initiative. The OKH promised another battalion of Tiger tanks and some more infantry divisions, but they proved too little and too late. Yet due to the muddy condition of the roads behind the front, Zhukov was forced to put off the resumption of his main offensive on the Proskurov–Chernovtsy axis for nine days, while supply columns struggled to restock the tank armies at the front. Unlike the Germans, Zhukov also ensured that a steady trickle of replacement troops and tanks reached the front line, replacing some of the losses incurred in the first phase of his offensive. Zhukov's left flank, less impaired by supply deficiencies because it relied on infantry armies, continued to inch forward across the Bug. The German XXXXVI Panzerkorps was tasked with creating a *feste Platz* in Vinnitsa and the city was defended by the 101. Jäger-Division and the 254. Infanterie-Division. Moskalenko was an experienced commander and he used his forces judiciously, efficiently supporting his four rifle divisions with a brigade of assault engineers and three regiments of SU-76 self-propelled guns. Rather than a frontal attack, Moskalenko used manoeuvres to approach Vinnitsa from the south and captured the critical rail junction at Zhmerynka on 18 March. Moskalenko's 38th Army conducted an assault crossing of the Bug River which outflanked most of the German defences in Vinnitsa, but it still took several days of heavy fighting to clear the city. By 1900hrs on 20 March, Polkovnik Aleksandr F. Vasilev's 305th Rifle Division had secured Vinnitsa. However, the Soviet troops were chagrined to find that Hitler's nearby *Werwolf* headquarters had been blown up by retreating German engineers, leaving no trophies for the victors. After the loss of Vinnitsa and Zhmerynka, a gap of more than 100km existed between Hube's 1. PzAOK and Wöhler's routed 8. Armee. The conditions were now ripe for Zhukov's 1st Ukrainian Front to encircle and annihilate Hube's army with one more major offensive.

The city of Vinnitsa was liberated by the Soviet 38th Army on 20 March after several days of heavy fighting. Note that all the major buildings on the street are burnt out and the American-made Willys Jeep in the foreground. (Author)

HUBE'S 1. PANZERARMEE IS ENCIRCLED, 21–26 MARCH 1944

In order to reinforce his main effort, Zhukov decided to shift Katukov's 1st Tank Army from his left flank (where it had played only a minor role in the first phase of the offensive) to his right flank. However, shifting Katukov's army nearly 200km would require several days, and in the meantime, General-leytenant Nikolay P. Pukhov's 13th Army was ordered to keep pushing against the 4. PzAOK forces between Tarnopol and Dubno. On 17 March, Dubno was captured, followed by Kremenets on 19 March, which put additional pressure on Raus' fragile army. Even as a few understrength units began to arrive to reinforce 4. PzAOK, Raus was forced to commit them immediately into the line to plug various gaps. Consequently, Balck's improvised front line was a crazy patchwork anchored upon a few strongpoints in towns and villages, but with wide open spaces in between. No tactical reserves of any kind were left.

At 0500hrs on 21 March, Cherniakhovsky's 60th Army opened a one-hour bombardment on the German positions between Tarnopol and Volochisk, the sector held by the 68. and 359. Infanterie-Divisionen. Cherniakhovsky was short of both infantry and artillery ammunition, but the German units opposing him were in worse condition. It was another cold, foggy morning, which hindered the artillery preparation. Then the two Soviet tank armies jumped off around 0600hrs, with Katukov's 1TA on the right and Badanov's 4TA on the left; altogether these formations had perhaps 400 operational tanks in four corps, supported by five rifle divisions. The Soviet tank armies advanced on a 22km-wide front, with the two tank corps (10GTC, 11GTC) advancing side by side in the centre while the two mechanized corps (6GMC, 8GMC) advanced on the outer flanks. The 68. Infanterie-Division, reinforced with a few tanks, bore the brunt of the enemy attack and was quickly overrun by the 10GTC and 11GTC. While the 8GMC pushed the 359. Infanterie-Division back toward Tarnopol, the 6GMC outflanked Mauss' 7. Panzer-Division positions near Skala. The SS-*LSSAH*, holding defensive positions behind the Bovenets' River, repulsed all enemy attacks on the first day of the offensive. By the end of the day, the two Soviet tank armies had advanced 25–28km and had ripped apart the tenuous connection between Raus' 4. PzAOK and Hube's 1. PzAOK. Balck claimed that his forces knocked out about 40 enemy tanks on this day, but even if true, this amounted to only 10 per cent of Zhukov's available armour in the crucial sector.

German situational awareness deteriorated rapidly as the Soviet armoured breakthrough accelerated and Balck issued a corps order on the night of 21/22 March that claimed that only 'isolated incursions' had occurred and that Katukov's 1st Tank Army had not achieved operational success. As a result, Balck initially ordered his subordinate divisions to hold fast, hoping to achieve the

Oberst Karl Mauss (left) was the commander of the 7. Panzer-Division during the Kamenets-Podolsky campaign and one of the key battlegroup leaders. Mauss came from a non-military background but proved himself as an infantry officer in World War I and then as a tactical leader in the campaigns of 1939–41. (Author)

The encirclement of Hube's 1. Panzerarmee, 20–26 March 1944

Legend:
- Approximate German front line, 23 March
- Soviet front line, 21 March

20 miles / 20km

1. 20 March: The Soviet 38th Army captures Vinnitsa.
2. 21 March: The 60th Army attacks the German positions between Tarnopol and Volochisk and achieves a breakthrough. Zhukov commits the 1st Tank Army and 4th Army into the breach.
3. 22 March: The 4th Guards Tank Corps pushes across the Seret River and envelops Tarnopol from the south. The garrison is encircled the next day.
4. 22 March: The 4th Tank Army isolates Kampfgruppe Mauss south of Volochisk.
5. 1st Guards Army increases pressure against the German forces holding Proskurov.
6. Hube shifts Breith's III. Panzerkorps to strengthen his vulnerable eastern flank.
7. 23 March: The 8th Guards Mechanized Corps (1TA) captures Chortkov.

8. 24 March: The 6th Tank Army succeeds in seizing a crossing over the Dniester near Mogilev-Podolsky.
9. The 1st Tank Army gains a crossing over the Dniester near Gorodenka.
10. Hube deploys a Kampfgruppe south of the Dniester to delay the 6th Tank Army.

11. 25 March: The lead tank brigade of 1st Tank Army reaches the northern outskirts of Chernovtsy but is not strong enough to capture the city.
12. 1700hrs: The Soviet 10GTC advances rapidly and fights its way into Kamenets-Podolsky.
13. 2100hrs: The XXIV Panzerkorps evacuates Proskurov.

14. 26 March: morning: The 38th Army captures Bar.
15. The 6th Tank Army captures Lipcani.
16. The 1st Tank Army sends a reinforced tank brigade to seize Khotin.

Place names: Vinnitsa, Zhmerynka, Mogilev-Podolsky, Staro-Konstantinov, Proskurov, Yarmolintsy, Dunaivtsi, Kamenets-Podolsky, Briceni, Lipcani (Lipkany), Chernovtsy, Khotin, Gorodok, Gusyatin, Gorodenka, Kolomya, Volochisk, Skala, Chortkov, Buchach, Tarnopol, Podgaytsy, Berezhany

Rivers: Sluch, Bug, Dniester, Smotrych, Zbruch, Seret, Strypa, Stryja

Unit labels: 18, 38, 40, 6, 371, 208, 17, 1, 254, 82, 101 Jäg, 168, III, 16, 20, 96, SS Reich, XXIV, 291, LIX, XXXXVI, 75, Pz, 1 Gd, 3 Gd, Mauss, 4 Gd, 60, 4, 1, 13

N

Soldiers from Hube's 1. Panzerarmee pass an empty aerial delivery cannister en route to the Strypa River. These cannisters, dropped by parachute, could deliver a maximum of 720kg of ammunition or about 400 litres of fuel. No food was parachuted to Hube's troops. (Author)

A column from the 16. Panzer-Division advances with SPWs and a PzKpfw IV tank. Like many of the units in Hube's Pocket, the 16. Panzer-Division could barely field a mixed Kampfgruppe with a handful of tanks and other AFVs. The rest of the division walked. (Author)

same kind of success that had stymied Zhukov's first offensive pulse. Balck was a highly competent battlefield commander but he operated under the same handicap as many other senior German officers at this stage of a lost war – namely, trying to put a positive spin on events in order to avoid the impression of defeatism. As a result of his decision, the 7. Panzer-Division was quickly outflanked by fast-moving Soviet armoured columns and forced to pull back 10km and refuse its left flank. The SS-*LSSAH* was also outflanked when Panfilov's 6th Guards Tank Corps (6GTC) broke through on its right flank. On 22 March, Katukov's 1TA advanced southward another 12km in spite of muddy roads and captured the town of Khorostkov. Poluboyarov's 4th Guards Tank Corps (4GTC) enveloped the 359. Infanterie-Division, pushed across the Seret River and widened the gaping hole in the XXXXVIII Panzerkorps' front. Balck received the s.Pz.Abt. 507 equipped with 51 brand-new Tiger tanks, which he used to reinforce the 357. and 359. Infanterie-Divisionen protecting the flanks of the Tarnopol garrison. However, within 48 hours, two Tigers had been destroyed and one-third of the remainder were non-operational.

Meanwhile, Badanov's 4TA applied heavy pressure against the 7. Panzer-Division and the SS-*LSSAH*, pushing them back. Initially, Mauss' 7. Panzer-Division had 12 attached Tigers from s.Pz.Abt. 503 but its Panzergrenadier units were extremely reduced by losses. Despite tenacious German resistance, Badanov's armoured spearheads kept forcing the 7. Panzer-Division to pull back and the SS-*LSSAH* had already lost its supply line to Yarmolintsy due to the advance of the 6GTC. By the afternoon of 22 March, the SS-*LSSAH* was reporting that its situation was 'untenable' and requested new orders from XXXXVIII Panzerkorps. Balck hesitated and it was not until 2055hrs that he accepted that his front was broken, and that retreat was the only option to save his divisions from annihilation. In his updated order, Balck designated the 7. Panzer-Division, SS-*LSSAH* and remnants of the 68. Infanterie-Division as Kampfgruppe Mauss but specified that it would remain under XXXXVIII Panzerkorps control – even though the group was now isolated from his corps headquarters near Tarnopol. Balck authorized a limited withdrawal but directed Kampfgruppe Mauss to hold a 17km-long sector from Satanov to Solomno. In fact, Soviet armour had already outflanked this line.

While Katukov's and Badanov's armour was flooding southward toward the Dniester, Zhukov ordered Grechko's 1st Guards Army (1GA) to

keep pressure on the LIX Armeekorps and Nehring's XXIV Panzerkorps at Proskurov. The main defence of the city rested upon a reinforced grenadier regiment from the 291. Infanterie-Division. German maintenance units in the city put in a Herculean effort to repair damaged tanks and other weapons, which partly revitalized the SS-*Das Reich* Kampfgruppe defending the eastern approaches to the city. The vulnerable south-west side of the city, threatened by Rybalko's 3GTA, was protected by the 19. Panzer-Division and a Kampfgruppe from the 11. Panzer-Division.[9] Zhukov also ordered Zhuravlev's 18th Army and Moskalenko's 38th Army to increase their attacks from the north-east and east, in order to push in Hube's vulnerable right flank. Hube responded by reassigning von der Chevallerie's LIX Armeekorps to hold the Yarmolintsy–Gorodok sector, south-west of Proskurov, and to try to maintain a link to Kampfgruppe Mauss. Nehring's XXIV Panzerkorps took over the defence of Proskurov and the northern part of the army's front line. In a display of German tactical agility, Breith's III Panzerkorps, which had been engaged in counterattacking Badanov's 4TA, was shifted east to assist Schulz's hard-pressed XXXXVI Panzerkorps. After the loss of Vinnitsa, Schulz was ordered to create a new 67km-wide eastern defence line between the town of Bar and the Dniester River, but he had only four depleted infantry divisions. In addition to Moskalenko's 38th Army, Konev's armies were also beginning to appear on Hube's right flank. Zhmachenko's 40th Army was already in contact with the XXXXVI Panzerkorps north of the Dniester and Kravchenko's 6th Tank Army was preparing to cross the Dniester at Mogilev-Podolsky. The 1. Panzerarmee was being pushed into a tight salient on the north side of the Dniester River, with only tenuous lines of communication to the south. In anticipation of a breakout to the south, Hube moved his headquarters to Kamenets-Podolsky, which sat astride the main road leading south to the Dniester. On 23 March, he also moved some of his support units south of the Dniester, to Khotin. Since Khotin possessed one of the few intact bridges over the Dniester, it was declared a *feste Platz* and Generalleutnant Josef Prinner (commander of Harko 311) was placed in command.

Once the Soviet armoured breakthrough occurred on both his flanks, Hube repeatedly asked von Manstein for permission to withdraw his army south of the Dniester and seek refuge behind the Carpathian Mountains. While this course of action had a fair probability of success in the short run and would likely save Hube's army from encirclement, von Manstein regarded it as an escape to nowhere. It would be difficult to supply 1. PzAOK in this remote corner of Romania or transport it to other sectors where it was badly needed. With Soviet armour already advancing south of the Dniester River, Hube's army would still be at risk of encirclement. Von Manstein

A platoon of light armoured cars from the 19. Panzer-Division waits in a village inside the Hube *Kessel*. Once the breakout began, it was critical for German recon units to find the best river crossing sites, identify enemy blocking positions and find gaps in the loose Soviet perimeter west of the Zbruch River. (Author)

9   The 11. Panzer-Division was assigned to the 8. Armee but some units were in the vicinity of Proskurov awaiting transfer to France for refit when the Soviet breakthrough occurred. One Kampfgruppe served with the 1. Pz.AOK during March–April 1944, including Major Karl von Sivers' I./Pz.Regt. 15, Pz.Gren.Regt. 110 and Pz.Pi.Btl. 209.

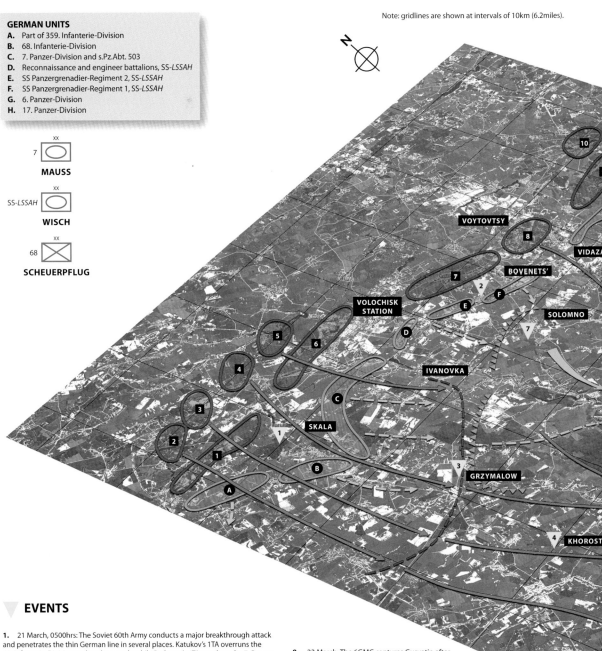

GERMAN UNITS

A. Part of 359. Infanterie-Division
B. 68. Infanterie-Division
C. 7. Panzer-Division and s.Pz.Abt. 503
D. Reconnaissance and engineer battalions, SS-*LSSAH*
E. SS Panzergrenadier-Regiment 2, SS-*LSSAH*
F. SS Panzergrenadier-Regiment 1, SS-*LSSAH*
G. 6. Panzer-Division
H. 17. Panzer-Division

XX
7 ⬭

MAUSS

XX
SS-*LSSAH* ⬭

WISCH

XX
68 ▢

SCHEUERPFLUG

VOYTOVTSY
VIDAZA
BOVENETS'
VOLOCHISK STATION
SOLOMNO
IVANOVKA
SKALA
GRZYMALOW
KHOROST

▼ EVENTS

1. 21 March, 0500hrs: The Soviet 60th Army conducts a major breakthrough attack and penetrates the thin German line in several places. Katukov's 1TA overruns the 68. Infanterie-Division and pushes south, while Badanov's 4TA envelops the 7. Panzer-Division.

2. 0600–1000hrs: The SS-*LSSAH* initially repulses attacks by the 18GRC across the Bovenets'.

3. Afternoon: The 7. Panzer-Division and remnants of the 68. Infanterie-Division withdraw and form a new line anchored on the town of Grzymalow.

4. 22 March: The 1TA continues to advance south, capturing Khorostkov, outflanking the 7. Panzer-Division.

5. Morning: The 6GTC penetrates the boundary between the SS-*LSSAH* and the 6. Panzer-Division, advancing rapidly south. The 6. Panzer-Division retreats to Yarmolintsy, breaking contact with the SS-*LSSAH*.

6. The 1. Panzer-Division moves to Gorodok to halt the advance of the 6GTC and to re-establish contact with the SS-*LSSAH*.

7. Evening: The SS-*LSSAH* retreats to form a new line, anchored on Solomno, facing both north and east. The SS-*LSSAH*, 7. Panzer-Division and 68. Infanterie Division are now designated as Kampfgruppe Mauss.

8. 23 March: The 6GMC captures Gusyatin after heavy fighting.

9. The 8GMC captures Chortkov.

10. 24 March: The SS-*LSSAH* covers the withdrawal of the 7. Panzer-Division across the Zbruch through Satanov.

11. After fending off Soviet attacks for a day, the SS-*LSSAH* withdraws to a new position at Zakupna, closer to the 1. Panzer-Division.

12. 25 March: The SS-*LSSAH* withdraws to Chemerovtsy.

13. The 10GTC bypasses Kampfgruppe Mauss and advances southeast toward Kamenets-Podolsky.

14. 26/27 March, evening: Under heavy enemy pressure, Kampfgruppe Mauss pulls farther south.

15. 28 March: The 1. Panzer-Division evacuates Gorodok and withdraws to the south.

16. 29 March: Kampfgruppe Mauss finally links up with elements of the 1. Panzer-Division near Lyantskorun.

THE ESCAPE OF KAMPFGRUPPE MAUSS, 21–29 MARCH 1944

The second phase of Zhukov's grand offensive quickly smashed through the thin front line held by the XXXXVIII Panzerkorps and isolated its two best mechanized divisions. However, Kampfgruppe Mauss conducted a fighting withdrawal over the course of nine days, moving 65km with minimal fuel, until it managed to link up with the rest of the 1. Panzerarmee.

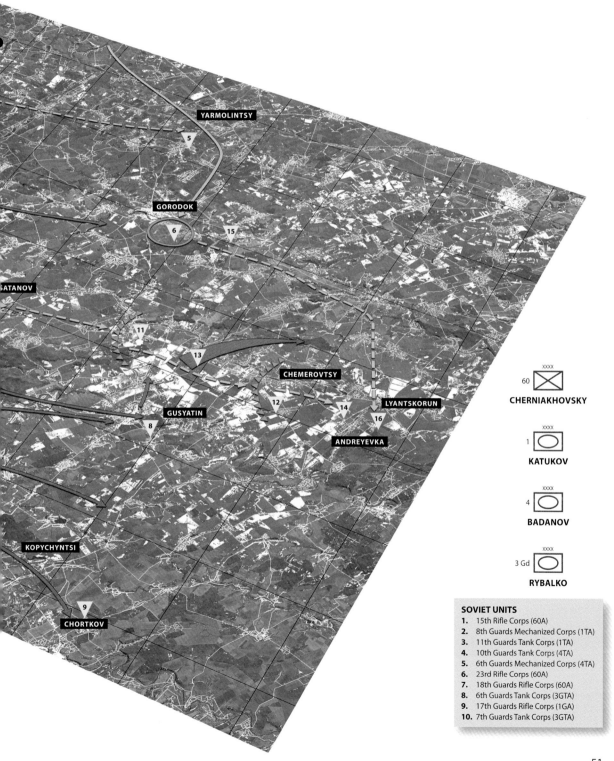

YARMOLINTSY

GORODOK

SATANOV

CHEMEROVTSY

LYANTSKORUN

GUSYATIN

ANDREYEVKA

KOPYCHYNTSI

CHORTKOV

60 ⊠ XXXX
CHERNIAKHOVSKY

1 ⬭ XXXX
KATUKOV

4 ⬭ XXXX
BADANOV

3 Gd ⬭ XXXX
RYBALKO

SOVIET UNITS
1. 15th Rifle Corps (60A)
2. 8th Guards Mechanized Corps (1TA)
3. 11th Guards Tank Corps (1TA)
4. 10th Guards Tank Corps (4TA)
5. 6th Guards Mechanized Corps (4TA)
6. 23rd Rifle Corps (60A)
7. 18th Guards Rifle Corps (60A)
8. 6th Guards Tank Corps (3GTA)
9. 17th Guards Rifle Corps (1GA)
10. 7th Guards Tank Corps (3GTA)

A column from the 19. Panzer-Division moves through a village during the breakout from the *Kessel*. The column has several PzKpfw IV tanks, passing some horse-drawn transport. (Author)

expected that Hube's army would be sidelined while Zhukov tore Raus' 4. Panzerarmee to pieces and advanced into south-east Poland. Instead, von Manstein concluded that a solution was needed that both saved Hube's army and enabled Heeresgruppe Süd to rebuild a new front line. If a retreat to the south would not serve the army group's operational requirements, then Hube would have to move to the west to link up with Raus. Thus, unlike the situation at Stalingrad, von Manstein concluded that attack, not defence, was the solution to this problem. It was a desperate solution and one that required a certain kind of commander to lead the breakout.

On 23 March, Katukov's armour continued to advance against minimal resistance and the 8GMC occupied the town of Chortkov, seemingly closing off any hope for Hube's 1. PzAOK to escape to the west. The 4GTC and two rifle corps from the 60th Army swung to the west and also succeeded in encircling the German garrison in Tarnopol, despite the presence of a company of Tiger tanks deployed to prevent this occurrence. Kampfgruppe Mauss was isolated near the town of Satanov, with most of Badanov's 4th Tank Army (6GMC, 10GTC) and three Soviet rifle divisions enveloping it from the south. Leytenant Evgeni Bessonov's battalion was part of the 6GMC attacks against Kampfgruppe Mauss, and he noted the heavy resistance from this isolated German formation. Altogether Mauss had about 40 operational AFVs, but the bedrock of the defence rested upon the remaining Tiger tanks of the s.Pz.Abt. 503, attached to Mauss' 7. Panzer-Division. The Luftwaffe also provided some valuable close air support and Bessonov stated that his battalion suffered heavy losses from enemy air attacks during this period. However, Kampfgruppe Mauss was desperately short of fuel and so four damaged Tigers had to be destroyed to prevent their capture. Late in the day, the 4. Panzerarmee finally agreed to transfer command of Kampfgruppe Mauss to the 1. Panzerarmee. In anticipation, Hube shifted Marcks' 1. Panzer-Division to Gorodok, in an effort to establish a link-up with Kampfgruppe Mauss. In Lvov, von Manstein bombarded the OKH with requests for reinforcements to prevent his beleaguered armies from disintegrating, as well as permission to withdraw from the most exposed positions.

The pace of the campaign picked up considerably on 24 March, as the Soviet armoured pincers began to close around Hube's 1. PzAOK. Konev's 2nd Ukrainian Front had succeeded in getting part of General-leytenant Andrei G. Kravchenko's 6th Tank Army across the Dniester near Mogilev-Podolsky, and small armoured battlegroups (some equipped with American-made M4A2 Sherman tanks) were already advancing westward. Hube hurriedly shifted Kampfgruppe Gollnick (elements of the 75. Infanterie-Division and the 18. Artillerie-Division, including some assault guns) south of the river to form a blocking position near Briceni (47km south-east of Khotin); these units managed to arrive just before the first Soviet tanks and were forced to fight a costly engagement. Fuel and ammunition shortages briefly halted Kravchenko's advance before he could smash his way through the improvised obstacle. In the west, the vanguard of Katukov's 1TA was approaching the Dniester, and by nightfall the first scouts from the 20th Guards Mechanized Brigade (8GMC) managed to cross the river in small boats at Ustechko, 12km north-east of Gorodenka.

By the next morning, Katukov had a motor rifle battalion across the Dniester and was getting ready to ferry across tanks from the 1st Guards Tank Brigade. In Lvov, von Manstein was tracking the battle and continued to urge Hube to withdraw to the west before he was completely encircled; at 1735hrs he sent a preliminary order to Hube, directing him to begin planning for a breakout to the west. Yet Hube was not sanguine about the idea of trying to fight his way through two Soviet tank armies with his own depleted formations, and instead continued to recommend a withdrawal into Romania via the Khotin bridgehead. At 1600hrs, Hitler ordered the 1. PzAOK to hold its current positions but authorized Hube to attack westward if he could re-establish connections with 4. PzAOK. Late that evening, von Manstein was ordered to report to the Führer.

By the morning of 25 March, as von Manstein prepared to fly to Berchtesgaden, Soviet armour was rapidly building up across the Dniester. From Moscow, the Stavka demanded that Zhukov and Konev complete the encirclement of Hube's army as soon as possible. Soviet pressure was also increasing against Hube's tightening perimeter north of the Dniester, compacting his forces. Arriving in time for the daily noon situation briefing at the Berghof, von Manstein recommended that Hube's army immediately attack westward to link up with 4. PzAOK and evacuate its current positions before it lost freedom of manoeuvre. Hitler refused to accept this assessment, claiming that Hube's forces were not in as much danger as von Manstein claimed. He also initially refused to release any reinforcements from the West and stated that no units could be released from occupation duty in Hungary due to 'political reasons'. However, after Hube again remonstrated with the OKH to approve his request to withdraw his army into Romania, Hitler finally relented. At the evening conference, Hitler authorized Hube to fight his way westward and agreed to transfer the II SS-Panzerkorps from France, along with two infantry divisions and another Tiger tank battalion, to provide a relief force. Von Manstein was satisfied and flew back to Lvov to begin planning the breakout operation. However, von Manstein had expended all his personal credit with Hitler, who was now determined to get rid of this argumentative Generalfeldmarschall.

Meanwhile, Zhukov's spearheads continued to close their grip around Hube's army. In the north, Nehring's XXIV Panzerkorps was under heavy pressure from Grechko's 1GA, and a salient had formed, anchored on Yarmolintsy, Proskurov and Bar. After Soviet tanks managed to cross the Yarmolintsy–Proskurov road and threatened to isolate the city, Hube was finally authorized to evacuate Proskurov. At dusk, the 291. Infanterie-Division evacuated the city. The Germans were forced to leave a great deal of immobilized equipment in the city, including roughly 50 Panther tanks awaiting repairs. The loss of Proskurov also meant the loss of its airfield and the nearby ammunition depot, which seriously reduced the 1. Panzerarmee's already fragile logistic situation. Farther south, Badanov's 4th Tank Army left

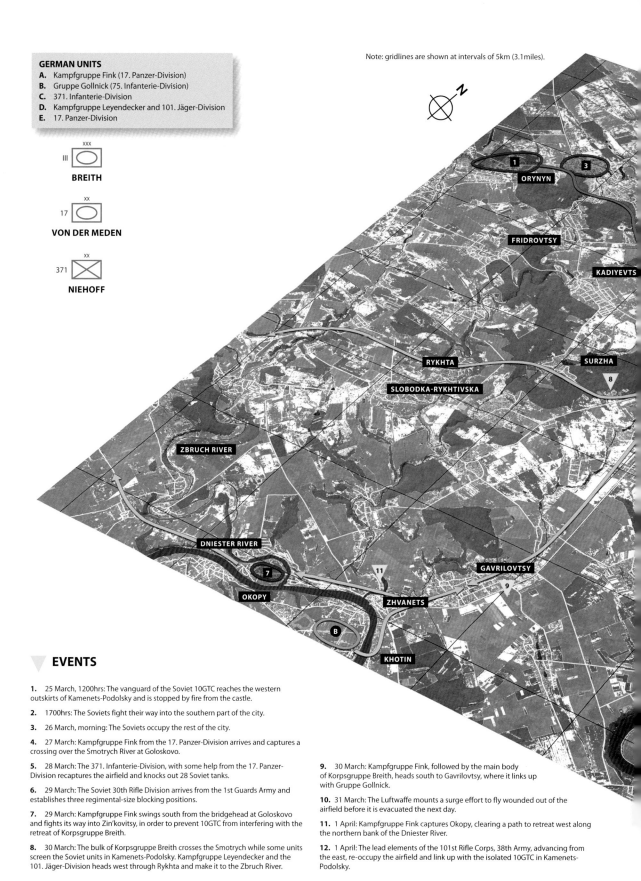

GERMAN UNITS

A. Kampfgruppe Fink (17. Panzer-Division)
B. Gruppe Gollnick (75. Infanterie-Division)
C. 371. Infanterie-Division
D. Kampfgruppe Leyendecker and 101. Jäger-Division
E. 17. Panzer-Division

BREITH

VON DER MEDEN

NIEHOFF

Note: gridlines are shown at intervals of 5km (3.1miles).

ORYNYN

FRIDROVTSY

KADIYEVTS

RYKHTA

SURZHA

SLOBODKA-RYKHTIVSKA

ZBRUCH RIVER

DNIESTER RIVER

GAVRILOVTSY

OKOPY

ZHVANETS

KHOTIN

▼ EVENTS

1. 25 March, 1200hrs: The vanguard of the Soviet 10GTC reaches the western outskirts of Kamenets-Podolsky and is stopped by fire from the castle.

2. 1700hrs: The Soviets fight their way into the southern part of the city.

3. 26 March, morning: The Soviets occupy the rest of the city.

4. 27 March: Kampfgruppe Fink from the 17. Panzer-Division arrives and captures a crossing over the Smotrych River at Goloskovo.

5. 28 March: The 371. Infanterie-Division, with some help from the 17. Panzer-Division recaptures the airfield and knocks out 28 Soviet tanks.

6. 29 March: The Soviet 30th Rifle Division arrives from the 1st Guards Army and establishes three regimental-size blocking positions.

7. 29 March: Kampfgruppe Fink swings south from the bridgehead at Goloskovo and fights its way into Zin'kovitsy, in order to prevent 10GTC from interfering with the retreat of Korpsgruppe Breith.

8. 30 March: The bulk of Korpsgruppe Breith crosses the Smotrych while some units screen the Soviet units in Kamenets-Podolsky. Kampfgruppe Leyendecker and the 101. Jäger-Division heads west through Rykhta and make it to the Zbruch River.

9. 30 March: Kampfgruppe Fink, followed by the main body of Korpsgruppe Breith, heads south to Gavrilovtsy, where it links up with Gruppe Gollnick.

10. 31 March: The Luftwaffe mounts a surge effort to fly wounded out of the airfield before it is evacuated the next day.

11. 1 April: Kampfgruppe Fink captures Okopy, clearing a path to retreat west along the northern bank of the Dniester River.

12. 1 April: The lead elements of the 101st Rifle Corps, 38th Army, advancing from the east, re-occupy the airfield and link up with the isolated 10GTC in Kamenets-Podolsky.

FIGHTING AROUND KAMENETS-PODOLSKY, 26 MARCH TO 1 APRIL 1944

The sudden capture of Kamenets-Podolsky by Badanov's 4th Tank Army came as a shock to Hube's 1. Panzerarmee. However, Badanov's armoured spearhead had shot its bolt and was essentially immobilized for a week and could not seriously interfere with Korpsgruppe-Breith's withdrawal across the Smotrych River.

BOLSHOYE ARMYANE

4

5

VERBKY

6

GOLOSKOVO

A

7

6

GUMENTSY

SHATAVA

4

C

ZIN'KOVITSY

DZAMCHE

1

2

TRAIN STATION

CASTLE

3

AIRFIELD

5

2

10

KAMENETS-PODOLSKY

12

8

SMOTRYCH RIVER

USTYA

DNIESTER RIVER

6 Gd XXX AKIMOV

10 Gd XXX BELOV

SOVIET UNITS
1. 49th Mechanized Brigade (part), followed by the 10th Guards Tank Corps (10GTC)
2. 61st and 63rd Guards Tank Brigades (10GTC), 29th Guards Motorized Brigade (10GTC)
3. 6th Guards Mechanized Corps Headquarters group, in Orynyn
4. 35th Rifle Regiment (30RD)
5. 71st Rifle Regiment (30RD)
6. 256th Rifle Regiment (30RD)
7. 17th Guards Mechanized Brigade
8. 101st Rifle Corps (38A)

most of General-leytenant Aleksandr I. Akimov's 6th Guards Mechanized Corps (6GMC) to pin down Kampfgruppe Mauss while Generalmajor Evtikhiy E. Belov's 10th Guard Tank Corps (10GTC) bypassed the SS-*LSSAH* positions and advanced rapidly on a straight path toward Kamenets-Podolsky. Hube had become so fixated on his northern and eastern flanks that he apparently failed to appreciate the threat approaching from the west until it was too late. The city was defended only by a small garrison of rear echelon troops. The main German defence was anchored on the 14th-century castle on the west side of the city, which dominated the main bridge over the Smotrych River.

Leytenant Evgeni Bessonov's company – reduced to just 35 soldiers mounted on three T-34s – was in the Soviet vanguard approaching Kamenets-Podolsky from the north-west. Bessonov's column was stopped by fire from the castle, so he sought an alternate crossing off to the south. By 1200hrs, the 61st Guards Tank Brigade and 29th Guards Motorized Brigade from Belov's 10GTC appeared on the western outskirts and began bombarding the German garrison in the castle, although the thick stone walls proved virtually impregnable. The Smotrych River itself proved a nearly insurmountable obstacle for the Soviet tanks, due to its very steep embankments. Nevertheless, by 1700hrs, the Soviets had begun to fight their way into the city, which caused the German support units to scatter and abandon vehicles. Hube evacuated his command post, but the Soviet troops became preoccupied with looting the large cache of German food and alcohol abandoned in the city. Next morning, the Soviets completed their occupation of the city centre and captured about 1,500 sick and wounded German personnel in the hospital, as well as large numbers of abandoned vehicles. There was little doubt that the sudden loss of Kamenets-Podolsky was a disaster for the 1. Panzerarmee.

At the same time, General-leytenant Andrei L. Getman's 11th Guards Tank Corps (11GTC) from 1TA was closing in on the city of Chernovtsy, one of Zhukov's primary objectives. The Axis garrison in the city was a jumble of quartermaster units, Flak troops, security personnel and even a battalion of Romanian border guards. Some combat units, including the 68. Infanterie-Division, 7. Panzer-Division and 25. Panzer-Division, had field replacement detachments in the city, equipped with small amounts of equipment. Indeed, a train loaded with 40 new Panther tanks and another with a battalion of replacement personnel were expected soon in the Chernovtsy rail station, but Getman's tankers arrived first. Polkovnik Nikolay V. Morgunov's 45th Guards Tank Brigade approached the city from the west around 1630hrs, while Podpolkovnik Ivan F. Boyko's 64th Guards Tank Brigade approached from the east. Two rifle regiments from the 24th Rifle Division also supported the attack. Boyko's brigade reached the northern outskirts of Chernovtsy around 2300hrs, which started a three-day fight for the inner city. Initially, Getman was not strong enough to take the city in a *coup de main*, nor was the German garrison cohesive enough to fend off an attack from two directions. Keeping his eye on the final objective, Getman also sent his 44th Guards Tank Brigade toward Khotin, to seize the critical bridge over the Dniester.

By the time that von Manstein arrived back in Lvov on the morning of 26 March, Hube's army had lost Proskurov and been run out of its headquarters at Kamenets-Podolsky. In the east, Moskalenko's 38th Army had captured Bar.

Chernovtsy was under attack, Soviet armour was approaching the bridge at Khotin and Kravchenko's 6th Tank Army had reached Lipcani on the Prut River. Hube's army was not yet encircled, but its ground lines of communication would be severed once Khotin was lost. Even aerial resupply would be difficult after the loss of the airfields at Proskurov and Kamenets-Podolsky; the Luftwaffe shifted its operations to the airfield located near Dunaivtsi. Hube responded to the loss of Kamenets-Podolsky by ordering Generalleutnant Karl-Friedrich von der Meden's 17. Panzer-Division to move immediately to recapture the city. Since von der Meden's division was about 30km away, near Dunaivtsi, it would take several days to reach the city in force, so Major Adolf-Oskar Fink's I./Pz.Regt. 63 and a few tanks were sent ahead as an advance unit. Hube also ordered Kampfgruppe Gollnick, withdrawing from Lipcani, to reinforce Generalleutnant Prinner's small garrison at Khotin.

Before dawn, von Manstein began issuing orders for the breakout operation to the west, and Luftflotte 4 was directed to begin a full-scale airlift operation to support Hube's army. Unlike Stalingrad, where the encircled 6. Armee had waited in vain for rescue, von Manstein was determined that the 1. PzAOK would fight its way out of encirclement. Accepting that escape to the south was now blocked, Hube quickly began issuing orders to his army to prepare for a mobile breakout operation to the west. The first task – a daunting one – was to establish crossings over the Zbruch River. If successful, Hube's 'wandering pocket' would then continue west another 67km until it linked up with a relief force from the 4. Panzerarmee on the Strypa River.

Hube still had plenty of troops and about 80 operational tanks (25 PzKpfw IV, 45 Panther, ten Tiger) and 60 assault guns. The real question was whether he had enough ammunition and fuel to fight his way through two Soviet tank armies. On 24 March, the 1. Panzerarmee's fuel reserves amounted to 665 tons (900 cbm) of petrol and 66 tons of diesel (90 cbm), not including fuel already carried on front-line vehicles. Ammunition was adequate for limited fighting, but artillery support would be minimal. The situation with food was not as good, with only four days' rations on hand. Luftflotte 4 was ordered to increase its airlift operations to support 1. Panzerarmee, but on 26 March, only 47 tons of supplies were flown into Dunaivtsi airfield, against a daily

A platoon (Zug) of PzKpfw IV tanks conducts a movement to contact across open, snow-covered terrain. Note that even though the terrain appears quite flat, visibility is limited to perhaps 1km. Consequently, most tank actions under these conditions could be expected to occur at ranges of just 600–800m. (Author)

One of the best German tactical transports was the *Raupenschlepper Ost* or RSO, which was specifically designed to operate in the primitive conditions encountered in Russia. Hube's 1. PzAOK used its RSOs to move fuel supplies and as prime movers for its remaining artillery. (Nik Cornish at www.stavka.photos)

A PzKpfw V Panther tank from the 1. Panzer-Division, apparently abandoned after a rollover incident. This type of hazard is not uncommon on icy roads and can inflict significant damage on the crew and their vehicle. (Author)

demand for 350 tons. Hube also had over 3,000 wounded soldiers awaiting evacuation at Dunaivtsi, but only 140 were flown out on the first night. In order to facilitate coordination between 1. PzAOK and Generalmajor Morzik's transport staff, a Luftwaffe signals detachment (equipped with four long-range radios) from the 7. Luftnachrichten-Regiment 38 under the command of a Hauptmann Hoffmann was flown in to Dunaivtsi. The Germans had learned a great deal about air-ground coordination at Stalingrad and Korsun, and now they intended to reap the benefits of that experience.

Although Zhukov appeared to be on the cusp of a major victory, circumstances were not as favourable as they might appear on the surface. While Badanov's 4th Tank Army had managed to capture Kamenets-Podolsky, it was reduced to fewer than 70 operational tanks, all of which were very low on ammunition and fuel. Furthermore, Belov's 10GTC and part of Akimov's 6th Guards Mechanized Corps (6GMC) were themselves isolated and incapable of further offensive action until resupplied. Rybalko's 3GTA was nearly fought out, reduced to just 60 operational tanks, with only the 9th Mechanized Corps still actively attacking. Katukov's 1st Tank Army, with about 130 operational tanks, was still combat-effective, but its 11GTC was still heavily engaged at Chernovtsy and Zhukov had given its other corps, the 8GC, a diverging secondary mission to go after Kolomya, in the region where the Hungarian VII Army Corps was beginning to assemble. Consequently, Zhukov's armour was quite dispersed, and he had no significant mobile reserve, just as the campaign was moving into its most critical phase. Nevertheless, Zhukov was convinced that the 1. Panzerarmee would either stay put in order to receive aerial resupply or attempt a breakout to the south, through Khotin. Konev's forces had also begun to reorient to the south-east, with Bogdanov's 2TA advancing toward Jassy and Kravchenko's 6TA temporarily pulled back into reserve. Only three rifle divisions from Zhmachenko's 40th Army were left to advance west along the southern bank of the Dniester, to complete the link-up with Katukov's armour near Khotin. Since Zhukov intended to get the lion's share of the credit for crushing the Kamenets-Podolsky pocket, he was satisfied that he did not need any further assistance from Konev's 2nd Ukrainian Front.

HUBE'S 1. PANZERARMEE BEGINS ITS BREAKOUT, 27 MARCH TO 5 APRIL 1944

After the loss of Kamenets-Podolsky on 26 March, Hube relocated his command post to the village of Mikhalovka, 12km south-west of Dunaivtsi. His first task was to pull together his scattered army and reorganize it for a breakout to the west. Most of his forces were facing north or east, fending off the attacks of the Soviet 1st Guards Army, 18th and 38th Armies.

On the western side of the army's perimeter, both Gruppe Mauss and the 1. Panzer-Division were isolated. Gruppe Gollnick was still located south of the Dniester, but in the process of pulling back to the Khotin bridgehead. Hube reorganized his army into two subordinate commands: Korpsgruppe Chevallerie (consisting of the LIX Armeekorps and the XXIV Panzerkorps) and Korpsgruppe Breith (consisting of the III Panzerkorps and XXXXVI Panzerkorps). As soon as possible, Korpsgruppe Chevallerie would link up with Gruppe Mauss and the 1. Panzer-Division and add them to its command. Hube's basic concept

A battery of abandoned German assault guns (the first two vehicles are StuG IVs but some in the rear are StuG IIIs) and a destroyed Marder tank destroyer near Proskurov, late March 1944. The fact that the assault guns are in column and appear undamaged is rather odd, suggesting that the crews abandoned the vehicles in haste. (Author)

for the breakout was a two-pronged parallel advance, with Chevallerie in the north and Breith in the south. However, the 1. Panzerarmee would also have to conduct a tenacious rearguard operation in the east, to prevent the Soviet 18th and 38th Armies from rolling up units as they began to withdraw. Given the urgency to break out before Zhukov could close in for the kill, Hube reckoned that he had just 48 hours to reorganize, redeploy and begin his operation, which meant there was no time for detailed planning. Hube's basic concept emphasized combat capabilities, which meant that support elements would not function in their normal manner.

Hube designated Korpsgruppe Chevallerie as his main effort and ordered it to establish a bridgehead over the Zbruch River at Skala-Podilska, which would be the main escape route for the 1. Panzerarmee. Korpsgruppe Breith was tasked with retaking Kamenets-Podolsky and then securing a secondary crossing, farther south, over the Zbruch. Nehring's XXIV Panzerkorps would provide the rearguard. German intelligence estimates from Heeresgruppe Süd assessed that Zhukov's armies had about 13–14 rifle divisions located between the Zbruch and Seret Rivers (which proved to be wildly exaggerated), plus elements of two tank armies. The terrain and weather were also serious complications, with wet, muddy conditions expected to reduce cross-country trafficability and make river crossings more time-consuming. Due to the shortage of fuel on hand, Hube issued an order that priority would go to combat vehicles; fuel was siphoned from damaged or inoperative vehicles. Furthermore, since only four-wheel drive and tracked vehicles were capable of moving cross-country under these conditions, a large amount of the motor transport would have to be abandoned or destroyed. Even most of the precious field kitchens (Gulaschkanonen) would have to be abandoned. An additional command dilemma was raised by the presence of 3,000 German wounded at the Dunaivtsi airfield. The Luftwaffe could evacuate only a fraction of this number before the airfield would have to be vacated and there would be little ground transport to move them, which could mean leaving the remaining wounded to the enemy.

Straight off, Hube's breakout operation got off to a poor start on 27 March. In the north, the 9th Mechanized Corps from Rybalko's 3GTA and Grechko's 1st Guard Army pushed back the LIX Armeekorps and captured the supply dumps at Yarmolintsy. Hube hoped that Gruppe Mauss would be able to

THE CROSSING OF THE ZBRUCH RIVER AT SKALA-PODILSKA, 31 MARCH 1944 (PP. 60–61)

On the evening of 29 March, the vanguard of 7. Panzer-Division captured intact a small bridge over the Zbruch River at Skala-Podilska **(1)**; this bridge was intended to be the primary escape route west for Korpsgruppe Chevallerie. Two days later, the main body of Korpsgruppe Chevallerie began to cross the bridge, although the column was moving at a crawling speed and consisted of a varied mix of armoured fighting vehicles, trucks, cars, horse-drawn wagons and marching troops **(2)**. Vehicles that were disabled or ran out of fuel were pushed off the road and some were set afire to prevent capture by the pursuing Red Army **(3)**. Most divisions began shedding their non-essential vehicles at the Zburch River crossing, but others would stagger along until the next river crossing. Since the Zbruch River was relatively shallow, a few tracked vehicles tried to ford the river, but some became stuck on its muddy banks **(4)**. The overall scene was reminiscent of Napoleon's retreat over the Berezina in 1812, with a fleeing army attempting to ford a water obstacle in order to reach safety, before it was cornered and destroyed by a vengeful foe.

Amazingly, Korpsgruppe Chevallerie was able to move all its formations across the Zbruch River in just a few days with minimal intereference from the enemy. The German ability to seize and hold river crossings for their main body to cross was one of the key reasons that Hube's 1. Panzerarmee succeeded in breaking out of the Kamenets-Podolsky *Kessel*.

hold its position 27km north-west of Kamenets-Podolsky as an assembly area for Korpsgruppe Chevallerie, but Mauss was under heavy pressure and forced to keep falling back. Likewise, the 1. Panzer-Division was forced to abandon Gorodok and retreat south to Smotrych, which enabled Grechko's 1GA to put additional pressure on Korpsgruppe Chevallerie. As a result, the German perimeter was contracting faster than Hube anticipated, and the enemy still clearly had the initiative. The only positive developments during the day were that the vanguard of von der Meden's 17. Panzer-Division

Kamenets-Podolsky in late March 1944, littered with abandoned German vehicles. The 14th-century castle in the background dominates the terrain around the Smotrych River. (Author)

reached the northern outskirts of Kamenets-Podolsky and managed to capture a small, intact bridge across the Smotrych River at Goloskovo (6km north of Kamenets-Podolsky), which would assist Breith's movements to the west. In addition, Gruppe Gollnick recrossed the Dniester and occupied a strong defensive position in Khotin. That evening, the Luftwaffe made a surge effort which managed to fly 45 tons of supplies into Dunaivtsi and flew out 208 wounded.

On the morning of 28 March, the weather reverted from partial thaw to freezing conditions. Hube issued a general order to his army: 'The 1. Panzerarmee will fight its way through the enemy and will defeat him where it meets him!' Korpsgruppe Chevallerie assembled most of its operational armour into Panzergruppe Waldenfels (under Generalmajor Rudolf von Waldenfels, the new commander of the 6. Panzer-Division), which had about 47 operational tanks (12 PzKpfw IV, 31 Panther, four Tiger) – this would be the battering ram to break through the Soviet encirclement. However, the battering ram had to get into position and that required moving about 40km from the area south-west of Yarmolintsy to the staging area near Lyantskorun, where it would link up with Gruppe Mauss. The movement proved extremely slow, and behind the Panzers the road was clogged with three side-by-side columns of motor transport. Four Tiger tanks from the s.Pz.Abt. 509 managed to fend off the pursuing 9th Mechanized Corps for a day, making a stand near the village of Tynna (17km north-west of Kamenets-

The vanguard of Bogdanov's 2nd Tank Army crossed the Dniester River near Yampol (135km south-east of Kamenets-Podolsky) on the morning of 17 March. Note the Valentine tank in the centre of the image. Bogdanov had barely a dozen tanks in this spearhead unit, including some Valentines. (Author)

Podolsky). It was at this point that Krasovskiy's 2VA appeared in force, using Il-2 Sturmoviks to bomb and strafe the densely packed German columns. Soviet Pe-2 bombers also struck one of the German fuel dumps at Dunaivtsi and destroyed 140 cbm of petrol (103 tons), about 15 per cent of the 1. PzAOK fuel reserves.

Breith was assisted in his efforts against Belov's 10th Guards Tank Corps (10GTC) in Kamenets-Podolsky by German interception of Soviet

Hube's breakout begins, 27 March–5 April 1944

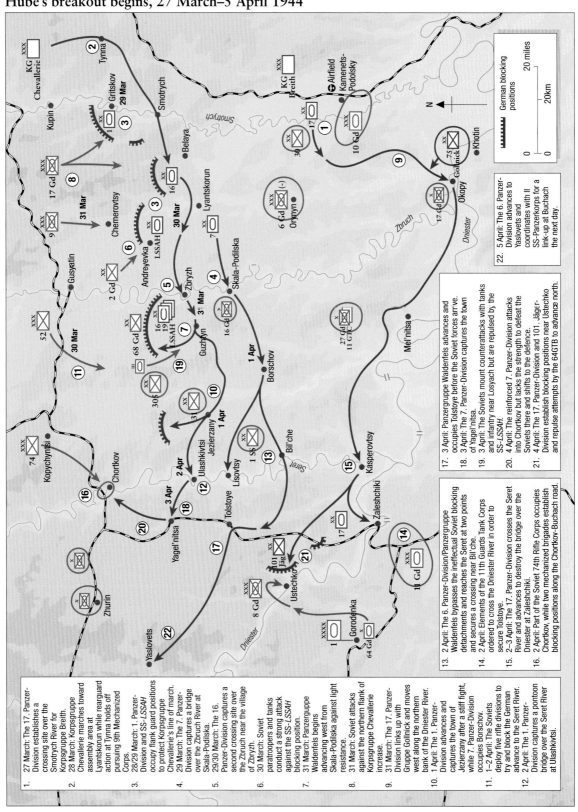

German blocking positions

| 0 | 20 miles |
| 0 | 20km |

1. 27 March: The 17. Panzer-Division establishes a crossing site over the Smotrych River for Korpsgruppe Breith.

2. 28 March: Korpsgruppe Chevallerie marches toward Lyantskorun while rearguard action at Tynna holds off pursuing 9th Mechanized Corps.

3. 28/29 March: 1. Panzer-Division and SS-LSSAH occupy flank guard positions to protect Korpsgruppe Chevallerie's line of march.

4. 29 March: The 7. Panzer-Division captures a bridge over the Zbruch River at Skala-Podilska.

5. 29/30 March: The 16. Panzer-Division captures a second crossing site over the Zbruch near the village of Zbrjzh.

6. 30 March: Soviet paratroopers and tanks conduct a strong attack against the SS-LSSAH blocking position.

7. 31 March: Panzergruppe Waldenfels begins advancing west from Skala-Podilska against light resistance.

8. 31 March: Soviet attacks against the northern flank of Korpsgruppe Chevallerie increase.

9. 31 March: The 17. Panzer-Division links up with Gruppe Gollnick and moves west along the northern bank of the Dniester River.

10. 1 April: The 1. Panzer-Division advances and captures the town of Jezierzany after a stiff fight, while 7. Panzer-Division occupies Borschov.

11. 1–2 April: The Soviets deploy five rifle divisions to try and block the German advance to the Seret River.

12. 2 April: The 1. Panzer-Division captures a pontoon bridge over the Seret River at Ulashkivtsi.

13. 2 April: The 6. Panzer-Division/Panzergruppe Waldenfels bypasses the ineffectual Soviet blocking detachments and reaches the Seret at two points and secures a crossing near Bil'che.

14. 2 April: Elements of the 11th Guards Tank Corps ordered to cross the Dniester River in order to secure Tolstoye.

15. 2–3 April: The 17. Panzer-Division crosses the Seret River and advances to destroy the bridge over the Dniester at Zaleshchiki.

16. 2 April: Part of the Soviet 74th Rifle Corps occupies Chortkov, while two mechanized brigades establish blocking positions along the Chortkov-Buchach road.

17. 3 April: Panzergruppe Waldenfels advances and occupies Tolstoye before the Soviet forces arrive.

18. 3 April: The 7. Panzer-Division captures the town of Yagel'nitsa.

19. 3 April: The Soviets mount counterattacks with tanks and infantry near Losyach but are repulsed by the SS-LSSAH.

20. 4 April: The reinforced 7. Panzer-Division attacks into Chortkov but lacks the strength to defeat the Soviets there and shifts to the defence.

21. 4 April: The 17. Panzer-Division and 101. Jäger-Division establish blocking positions near Ustechko and repulse attempts by the 64GTB to advance north.

22. 5 April: The 6. Panzer-Division advances to Yaslovets and coordinates with II SS-Panzerkorps for a link-up at Buchach the next day.

radio traffic from the isolated units in the city, providing valuable insight into enemy dispositions and their miserable supply situation. Thanks to this intelligence windfall, von der Meden's partially assembled 17. Panzer-Division was able to conduct a hasty attack which claimed to have knocked out 29 Soviet tanks, leaving Belov with less than 15 operational tanks. Kampfgruppe Fink and elements of the just-arriving 371. Infanterie-Division recaptured the airfield, which was soon put back into use to fly in more fuel and ammunition. Three regiments of the Soviet 30th Rifle Division arrived from the approaching 1GA in the north but proved unable to stop the Germans from crossing the Smotrych River and swinging south-west to envelop the remaining Soviet forces in Kamenets-Podolsky. Despite this enemy activity, Zhukov was not unduly concerned about local German counterattacks, since Soviet intelligence assessed that Hube's army would try to escape via Khotin into northern Romania. Thus, Zhukov was focused on closing off the southern escape route and did not see any urgency in reinforcing Soviet blocking forces along the Zbruch River. Instead, he was encouraged that Dremov's 8GMC (from 1TA) was running wild south of the Dniester, capturing the city of Kolomya and routing a division from the Hungarian VII Army Corps.

During the night of 28/29 March, Korpsgruppe Chevallerie established tentative contact with Gruppe Mauss near Lyantskorun. Chevallerie was moving toward the assembly area along the *Rollbahn* (main supply route) from Tynna through Smotrych, and he ordered the SS-*LSSAH* and Kampfgruppe Scheuerpflug (68. Infanterie-Division) to protect the northern flank of the assembly area. Marcks' 1. Panzer-Division was tasked with protecting the right flank of the *Rollbahn* at Gritskov, on the Smotrych River. As a preliminary requirement, Chevallerie ordered Mauss' 7. Panzer-Division to advance west and seize a bridgehead over the Zbruch at Skala-Podilska. At 0530hrs on 29 March, Mauss began advancing, which signalled the beginning of Hube's breakout effort. Mauss discovered that there were surprisingly few Soviet troops in the Skala-Podilska sector, mostly just support units from Badanov's 4th Tank Army. Consequently, even the weak 7. Panzer-Division was able to capture the small bridge over the Zbruch and the town by nightfall. Before Badanov could react to the loss of Skala-Podilska, he became caught up in the fighting around Kamenets-Podolsky and was evacuated after he was badly wounded by an explosion. Consequently, not only were the 4TA's lines of communication severed, but its command and control was also disrupted at a key moment. The result was that Korpsgruppe Breith gained the tactical initiative at Kamenets-Podolsky over the inert 10GTC, which greatly improved the odds of a successful breakout. Meanwhile, Chevallerie was pushing forces down the *Rollbahn* as fast as he could, and Generalmajor Hans-Ulrich Back's 16. Panzer-Division was in the lead, reaching Lyantskorun during the afternoon; along the way he managed to scoop up an unwary battery of Soviet heavy howitzers. During the night, Back sent his reconnaissance battalion forward to seize another crossing over the Zbruch at Zbryzh, 7km north of Skala-Podolsky.

As yet, Zhukov failed to recognize that Hube was beginning a breakout operation to the west, despite reported skirmishing along the Zbruch River. Grechko's 1GA, with some assistance from the 9th Mechanized Corps (which had been temporarily detached from 3GTA to support 1GA), was making steady progress pushing the LIX Armeekorps south, which worried Hube.

An armour column from Getman's 11GTC (1TA) crossing the Dniester River via a ford, approximately 25 March 1944. The lead vehicle is an SU-85 assault gun, followed by two T-34 Model 1943 tanks. Note the commander's cupola on the T-34s – a feature belatedly added to enhance situational awareness. (Author)

Likewise, the 18th and 38th Armies were also advancing, slowly but steadily, toward Dunaivtsi. Zhukov decided to pull the rest of Rybalko's 3GTA back into reserve to refit, which actually left him with very little armour north of the Dniester River. Badanov's 4th Tank Army (temporarily led by Belov) was virtually immobilized between Kamenets-Podolsky and Orynyn, and units like Leytenant Bessonov's motorized rifle battalion were reduced to just 60 soldiers. Unaware of 4TA's plight, Zhukov felt that situation would be cleared up forthwith. Besides, reports from Katukov's 1st Tank Army were quite satisfactory, with Chernovtsy finally secured by Getman's 11GTC. Once refuelled, Zhukov expected Katukov's tankers to continue their rampage south of the Dniester, so he was in a bullish mood. In contrast, Hube recognized that one serious mistake would likely result in failure of the breakout operation and the destruction of his army. Zhukov was playing for glory, while Hube was fighting for survival – a key difference in command outlook.

The next day, 30 March, Korpsgruppe Chevallerie continued to plod toward the assembly area at Lyantskorun. Due to heavy enemy pressure coming from the north and north-west, Chevallerie was obliged to detach units to act as covering force detachments to prevent the enemy from severing the *Rollbahn*. Both the SS-*LSSAH* and 1. Panzer-Division served as flank guards, fending off enemy probes, mostly from the 17th Guards Rifle Corps (1GA). Grechko committed some of his independent armour units, including some with heavy tanks, to assist the 2nd Guards Airborne Division in an attack, which hit the SS-*LSSAH* hard. Furthermore, Nehring's XXIV Panzerkorps was conducting a phased withdrawal to cover the rear of Korpsgruppe Chevallerie from Zhuravlev's 18th Army. Surprisingly, the Soviets still had negligible forces near the lightly held 7. Panzer-Division bridgehead over the Zbruch; a serious counterattack at this time and place might have seriously disrupted Hube's breakout plan. By this point, Zhukov was beginning to notice that German forces were shifting westward, and he ordered Grechko to send the 52nd and 74th Rifle Corps to create blocking positions along the Zbruch, but this proved too late.

Another view of the same 11GTC column fording the Dniester River. Note the abandoned German Sd.Kfz. 250 half-track, an Sd.Kfz. 11 3-ton half-track and several cars in the river. Also note that the SU-85 assault gun is carrying extra fuel drums. (Author)

Farther south, Breith left screening forces to keep an eye on the isolated 10GTC units in Kamenets-Podolsky while the bulk of his Korpsgruppe slipped across the Smotrych River, then proceeded south to link up with Gruppe Gollnick. The overcast skies and frequent snow showers helped to partly conceal the German columns from Soviet aerial reconnaissance, which made it difficult for Zhukov to ascertain Hube's intentions.

In fact, the main drama of the day occurred not at the front, but in von Manstein's headquarters in Lvov. That morning, he was peremptorily ordered to fly back again to Berchtesgaden, where Hitler relieved him of command. Hitler told him that Generalfeldmarschall Walter Model would take his place and that Heeresgruppe Süd would be split into Heeresgruppe Nordukraine (to command 1. PzAOK, 4. PzAOK and the Hungarian 1st Army) and Heeresgruppe Südukraine (to command the remnants of Wöhler's 8. Armee and 17. Armee in the Crimea). Von Manstein's removal should not have been a surprise, since he had suffered one defeat after another for the past nine months and was openly critical of Hitler's decision-making.

A Soviet SU-76 self-propelled gun passes an abandoned German 8.8cm Flak gun in the streets of Chernovtsy. The city finally fell to Katukov's 1st Tank Army on 29 March 1944, after several days of hard fighting. (Author)

On 31 March, Hube's breakout operation began to gather momentum as the weather shifted back to daily snow showers. Each division led with combat units out front in a *Stossgruppe* (shock group), followed by their artillery and then their support troops. Even before Korpsgruppe Chevallerie crossed the Zbruch, German divisions began to mix their troops in Kampfgruppen, which gathered up operational AFVs and the remaining infantrymen. Rather than have all traffic try to squeeze over the one permanent bridge near Skala-Podilska, the 16. Panzer-Division managed to build an improvised bridge at Zbryzh, although it was not strong enough to support tanks. Consequently, all of Gruppe Chevallerie's tanks were limited to the Skala-Podilska bridge, which would have made an excellent target for Soviet bombers, had not falling snow reduced visibility to near zero. By the end of the day, Hube had a substantial force across the Zbruch, including a good portion of Panzergruppe Waldenfels. His advance guard had pushed forward to capture the village of Guzhtyn, eliminating a small Soviet blocking unit. On the eastern side of Hube's shifting perimeter, the 168. Infanterie-Division evacuated Dunaivtsi just as the 18th Army arrived. The SS-Kampfgruppe *Das Reich* was virtually out of fuel and forced to abandon most of its motor vehicles and heavy equipment, leaving it little more than a 'leg' infantry unit. Since the airfield at Kamenets-Podolsky was also going to be evacuated shortly, the Luftwaffe made one last surge effort, using 57 Ju 52s to fly in more fuel and ammunition and then fly out 830 wounded.

The next day, 1 April, began as another cloudy day, with significant snowfall. The 1. Panzer-Division led the advance with a mixed *Stossgruppe* under Oberstleutnant Heinz-Werner Frank, comprising 11 Panthers and two small battalions of Panzergrenadiers. Frank's group moved 16km to assault the village of Jezierzany by late afternoon.[10] A regimental-size group from the 316th Rifle Division, reinforced with an artillery battalion and about 20 T-34 tanks, had already reached the village and established a strong blocking position east of the town. Around 1730hrs, Frank's lead elements encountered a screen of 45mm anti-tank guns, but pulled back due to intense fire. Frank sent an assault group off to try and hit from the north,

10 Modern Ozeryany.

Elements of Kravchenko's 6th Tank Army crossing the Prut River on pontoons, late March 1944. Note the Valentine tank on the pontoon, with extra fuel drums on the rear deck. Kravchenko's rapid advance complicated Hube's plan to withdraw south into Romania, since Soviet armour was already along his intended line of retreat. (Author)

but encountered T-34 tanks. After several hours of skirmishing, Frank shifted to the left and sent a battalion to conduct a night attack against the southern end of the village around 2030hrs, which apparently caught the Soviets by surprise. After some sharp fighting, the Soviet defence collapsed and the survivors withdrew, leaving Kampfgruppe Frank to secure Jezierzany; the Germans claimed to have destroyed six T-34 tanks, 20 45mm anti-tanks and 13 76mm field guns, plus 32 prisoners taken. The Panzergrenadier-Regiment 1 suffered seven killed and 36 wounded in this action and several German tanks were knocked out, but the Soviet roadblock had been removed.

Pausing for only a few hours to rest in Jezierzany, Stossgruppe Frank continued to advance toward its next objective – the Seret River – during the night of 1/2 April. Major Ernst Lösch, commander of the I./Panzergrenadier-Regiment 1, led a sub-detachment built around his battalion and a few Panther tanks. Lösch reached the village of Ulashkivtsi (Ułaszkowce) at 0345hrs; his scouts discovered the existence of an intact 60-ton bridge over the Seret River, but an enemy battalion-size force (probably from the 141st Rifle Division) occupied the village. Judging that the Soviets in the village were not expecting a night attack in a snowstorm, Lösch decided to rely upon surprise. The German Panzergrenadiers quietly moved in on foot and successfully captured the bridge at a cost of 19 casualties, while two T-34s guarding the bridge were knocked out by the Panthers. By 0615hrs, Lösch had secured the area around the bridge and signalled his success to the 1. Panzer-Division. Parallel to the 1. Panzer-Division, the 7. Panzer-Division and 20. Panzergrenadier-Division captured the town of Borschov, a vital road hub in this sector. Although making good forward progress – about 30km in two days – Korpsgruppe Chevallerie was forced to employ the 16., 19. and SS-*LSSAH* Panzer-Divisionen to protect the right flank of the breakthrough corridor from probing by Grechko's 1GA.

Farther back, Korpsgruppe Breith had evacuated the Kamenets-Podolsky airfield and begun a fighting withdrawal to the Zbruch River. Gruppe Gollnick evacuated the Khotin bridgehead and joined Breith's withdrawal. Breith had much less armour than Chevallerie and he used von der Meden's 17. Panzer-Division and the 101. Jäger-Division as his advance guard, while the SS-*Das Reich* and five infantry divisions formed the rearguard. Von der Meden's 17. Panzer-Division advanced westward along the northern bank of the Dniester, where it discovered there were very few Soviet forces. Indeed, the only significant enemy force that stood in its way was Polkovnik Mikhail V. Medvedev's 17th Guards Mechanized Brigade (17GMB) from the 6GMC, which was deployed in a superb blocking position at Okopy. At this point, Medvedev's brigade overlooked a bridge over the 50m-wide Zbruch River, with excellent fields of fire. The Dniester River was on Medvedev's right flank and the Zbruch served as a moat around the village, which meant that the Germans could not manoeuvre around this position – they had to go straight in. Another mechanized brigade, the 16GMB, was 20km farther west, at Mel'nitsa. However, the Soviet leadership was getting jumpy after Korpsgruppe Breith slipped past 10GTC at Kamenets-Podolsky and was uncertain in which direction it was heading, so someone in the chain of command ordered the two mechanized brigades to detach subunits to cover other possible enemy routes, such as Germankovka. Consequently, by the time that Major Fink's Kampfgruppe from the 17. Panzer-Division reached Okopy, Medvedev's brigade had been weakened and was looking over its shoulder, suspecting it had been bypassed. The 17. Panzer-Division apparently caught Medvedev by surprise and brusquely shoved his blocking detachment aside, thereby gaining a critical crossing over the Zbruch for the rest of Korpsgruppe Breith. Although Zhukov had managed to redeploy elements of five Soviet rifle divisions (along with some independent tank regiments and some corps-level artillery and anti-tank guns) east of the Seret River by the end of 1 April, none of these blocking detachments succeeded in inflicting any serious delay upon the advance of Hube's 1. Panzerarmee.

On the morning of 2 April, Hube's 1. Panzerarmee occupied a perimeter that measured approximately 43km by 32km, with the army command post in Borschov. Panzergruppe Waldenfels was just west of Borschov, where it faced only minor opposition from small blocking detachments of the Soviet 4th Tank Army. Thanks to the Luftwaffe liaison teams, Luftflotte 4 was able to airdrop some ammunition and fuel to the advance units, but just enough to keep the tanks and a few combat support vehicles operational. With Stossgruppe Frank already on or near the Seret River, Chevallerie ordered Panzergruppe Waldenfels to advance toward the Seret as well, using a route farther south. Waldenfels sent two reconnaissance groups forward to the river, one toward the village of Bil'che (Bilcze) with Kampfgruppe Hauschildt following close behind, and the other toward Lisovtsy, with Kampfgruppe Stahl following. Kampfgruppe Keller, primarily from the 11. Panzer-Division, also headed toward Bil'che.[11] Polkovnik Ilya V. Kaprov's 155th Rifle Division had already occupied blocking positions in the villages of Glubichek and Pen'ki, which controlled the main road network leading west to the Seret River. However, Kaprov's division lacked any real support and was virtually out of ammunition, so Waldenfels easily brushed past this useless roadblock by 1330hrs. Three T-34s attached to Kaprov's infantry were easily dispatched by a platoon of Hornisse tank destroyers. En route to the river, two Tigers fell out with mechanical problems and one was lost to enemy action, leaving just two operational. Nevertheless, Panzergruppe Waldenfels reached Bil'che and gained a crossing over the Seret by about 2100hrs. Thus, by the end of 2 April, Hube's vanguard had secured two separate crossing sites across the Seret.

Despite these German tactical successes, Zhukov was beginning to react to the breakout. Dremov's 8GMC from Katukov's 1TA was far to the west,

---

11 KG Hauschildt consisted of Pz.Gren.Regt. 4, I./Pz.Regt. 15, I./Pz.Art.Regt. 76 and a company of engineers. KG Stahl consisted of Pz.Gren.Regt. 114, s.Pz.Jg.Abt. 88 [Hornisse], two batteries of towed artillery and one company of engineers. KG Keller consisted of Pz.Gren.Regt. 110, one battery of towed artillery, one engineer company and a Flak battalion.

Panzerarmee rearguard actions, 27 March–5 April 1944

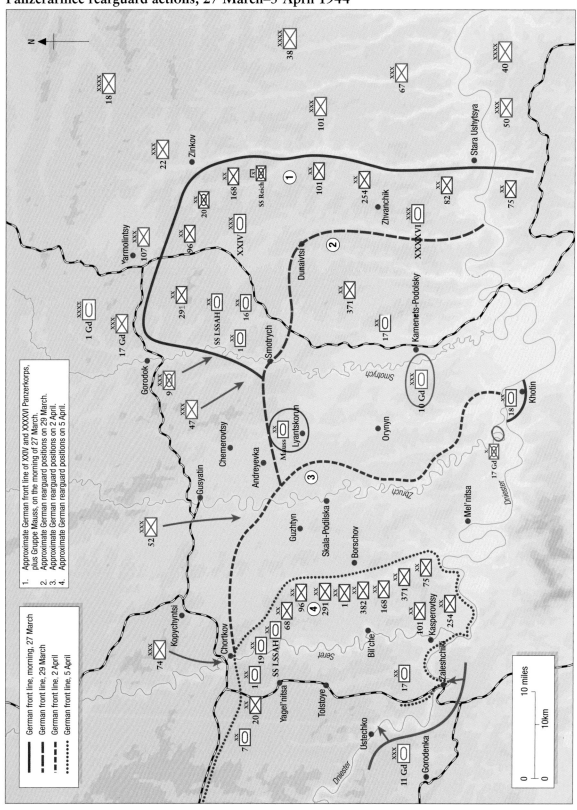

70

outside the city of Stanislav (now Ivano-Frankivsk), but parts of Getman's 11GTC were near Gorodenka; Zhukov ordered Katukov to send Getman's corps back across the Dniester, and two tank brigades (40, 45) began crossing on 2 April. The 11GTC would occupy a blocking position near Tolstoye (Tovste).[12] Zhukov also ordered reinforcements sent to the critical city of Chortkov, which dominated the road network west of the Seret River. By late on 2 April, the 141st and 183rd Rifle Divisions were in or near Chortkov and another rifle division (276) and a mechanized rifle brigade were en route. Elements of two mechanized brigades from the 6GMC (4TA) – which had been wandering around in search of a mission after failing to prevent Korpsgruppe Breith from getting across the Zbruch River – were now assigned to establish blocking positions west of Chortkov, to control the route west to Buchach. With strong blocking positions established at Tolstoye and Chortkov, Zhukov expected that he could halt Hube's breakout attempt until more infantry arrived. However, Zhukov failed to understand the wastage that had occurred in his front-line units, and the Germans reported that many of the blocking positions they encountered were merely small groups of infantry and a few tanks.

Zhukov also chose to issue a clumsy surrender demand to Hube's encircled forces; at 1000hrs on 2 April, a Soviet radio signal *en clair* in German was broadcast. The message stated, 'You cannot get out of the pocket', and stipulated that any units that did not surrender by the end of the day would face summary execution of every third soldier. Zhukov's crude intimidation demonstrates his degree of frustration and served only to instil further fighting spirit in the soldiers of the 1. Panzerarmee, who now knew it was victory or death. Over the course of the following days, propaganda leaflets with similar ultimatums were airdropped over the 'wandering pocket', with no effect.

At this point, the Kamenets-Podolsky campaign becomes an excellent example of the OODA (Observe-Orient-Decide-Act) loop, an American military concept developed in the 1990s. Zhukov observed the German breakout, began to reorient his forces, made his decision where to disrupt the breakout and began to act by 1–2 April. However, Hube's forces 'got inside Zhukov's OODA loop' – in modern military parlance – by reacting more quickly than Zhukov did, which enabled the German forces to seize the initiative. Before Zhukov's blocking forces could reach either Tolstoye or Chortkov in strength, Hube's vanguard arrived in both locations first.

On the morning of 3 April, Panzergruppe Waldenfels crossed the Seret at Bil'che and advanced to occupy Tolstoye before Katukov's tank brigades arrived. Two German assault guns were lost in the town and the last two Tigers broke down, but Waldenfels had secured a strong position to support the advance to the Strypa River. Waldenfels decided to spend the next day at Tolstoye, repairing some of his damaged tanks, while the rest of the 6. Panzer-Division caught up.

At the same time, Stossgruppe Frank (reinforced with elements of the 7. Panzer-Division) advanced from its bridgehead and captured the village of Jagielnica (Yagel'nitsa), 9km south of Chortkov. At this point, the Germans became aware from radio intercepts and Luftwaffe reconnaissance that Zhukov was sending strong reinforcements to Chortkov, from where

---

12 Referred to as 'Tluste Miasto' on German maps.

they could attack into the flank of Korpsgruppe Chevallerie as it tried to advance west to the Strypa River. Chevallerie ordered Marcks' 1. Panzer-Division to attack Chortkov in order to disrupt the Soviet threat from this quarter. On the morning of 4 April, Stossgruppe Frank advanced boldly toward Chortkov with 12 tanks (seven Tigers and five PzKpfw IV), three very depleted Panzergrenadier battalions and a reconnaissance battalion. A Soviet tank-infantry blocking detachment was eliminated south of the town, with five T-34s shot up by the Tigers. By 1145hrs, Frank was attacking into the western side of Chortkov, but ran into strong resistance from the 141st Rifle Division. Although the Germans attempted to push their way into the city with house-to-house fighting, Major Lösch was wounded, and it was obvious that Frank lacked the infantry strength to prevail. Instead, Chevallerie ordered the 1. and 7. Panzer-Divisionen to destroy the bridges over the Seret at Chortkov and prevent Soviet units from arriving from the north to attack into the flank of the breakout corridor. Frank managed to destroy the railroad bridge, but succeeded only in damaging the two road bridges. Chevallerie ordered Marcks to shift to the defence and sent the 20. Panzergrenadier-Division to reinforce the flank guard at Chortkov.

The weather had changed again, with temperatures increasing to 42°F (8°C), which turned the roads back into muddy quagmires. Waldenfels was eager to resume the march to the Strypa River but he had to repeatedly fend off small-scale enemy counterattacks at Tolstoye and he was short of fuel. Nevertheless, on the morning of 5 April, Major Paul Stahl, commander of Panzergrenadier-Regiment 114, set out with his infantry mounted on the remaining trucks, a few tanks and a platoon of six Hornisse tank destroyers. Stahl was able to reach the village of Yaslovets, 12km south-east of Buchach, the expected link-up point with the 4. Panzerarmee. A Luftwaffe liaison team embedded with Stahl's battlegroup requested an aerial resupply drop, and a load of fuel was delivered by parachute, ensuring that the vanguard could reach the objective the next day. Hube's breakout operation was about to reach its climax.

Meanwhile, the bulk of Korpsgruppe Chevallerie's main body was still located between the Zbruch and Seret rivers. Most of the slow-moving Korpsgruppe Breith was still in the process of crossing the Zbruch at Okopy or at another site farther north, but von der Meden's 17. Panzer-Division skirted along the northern bank of the Dniester and crossed the Seret on 4 April. Breith ordered von der Meden to prevent interference from enemy armour south of the Dniester, so he sent Kampfgruppe Fink to destroy the railroad bridge at Zaleshchiki, which was accomplished. After that, the 17. Panzer-Division advanced west to screen Katukov's crossing site over the Dniester at Ustechko. Breith sent the 101. Jäger-Division and 18. Artillerie-Division to reinforce the 17. Panzer-Division. Thus, Breith was prepared to deal with any Soviet armour attempting to cross the river.

By 4 April, most of the enemy attacks on Hube's pocket were coming from Grechko's 1GA in the north. The SS-LSSAH fended off several counterattacks north of Borschov, but it had lost all its artillery. Zhuravlev's 18th Army and Moskalenko's 38th Army were pursuing slowly from the west, but the detachment of three rifle corps from them to reinforce the Seret River line had considerably reduced their combat power. Lacking significant operational reserves, Zhukov was robbing from Peter to pay

Paul. Furthermore, virtually all of Zhukov's front-line units were suffering from serious supply shortages, particularly ammunition. If Hube's army had remained stationary and opted to fight a defensive action, this would not have mattered much, but Zhukov's formations were not logistically prepared to fight a protracted mobile battle. Another complication was the issue of command and control – who was responsible for stopping Hube's breakout attempt? Zhukov simply assigned Rybalko's 3GTA and Leliushenko's 4TA to control the fight around Chortkov, while Katukov's 1TA would control operations along the southern Seret River. However, the rifle divisions assigned to occupy blocking positions along the Seret River were from multiple formations and arrived piecemeal, often with no clue what was going on in this sector. Consequently, the Soviet response to Hube's breakout was poorly coordinated.

While the generals on both sides planned their next move, Hube's exhausted soldiers continued to retreat through the snow and the mud, hoping to reach sanctuary across the Strypa River. Many soldiers retreated on foot or in horse-drawn Panjewagons; only the severely wounded were allowed to ride on the remaining motor transport. The columns had very little in the way of rations and most soldiers were fortunate if they received a slice of bread per day. Even potable water was in short supply. On 4 April, the Luftwaffe managed to temporarily open airstrips at Borschov and Yagel'nitsa, which enabled over 200 tons of ammunition and fuel to be flown in directly over the course of two nights. Yet the Soviet 2VA did not seriously interfere with the German airlift operations, and even air attacks on the retreating columns had subsided.

THE ESCAPE OF 1. PANZERARMEE, 6–9 APRIL 1944

The ultimate fate of Hube's 1. Panzerarmee hinged upon a timely link-up with a relief force provided by Raus' 4. Panzerarmee. After Hitler authorized the transfer of SS-Obergruppenführer Paul Hausser's II SS-Panzerkorps from Holland on 25 March, the Waffen-SS troops began fast transport to the Eastern Front. Just eight days after receiving the transfer order, the lead elements of Hausser's corps began detraining in Lvov. Yet neither the 9. nor the 10. SS-Panzer-Divisionen was complete, since their Panther battalions were still in training and they had to substitute assault gun battalions instead. Both divisions were also missing their Panzerjäger-Abteilungen and some support troops. Most of the SS troops had not even been issued winter uniforms. Nevertheless, the II SS-Panzerkorps was a potent combined arms force that added 98 PzKpfw IV tanks and 88 StuG assault guns to Raus' tattered command, along with fresh battalions of SS-Panzergrenadiers. Hausser's II SS-Panzerkorps would also be reinforced with the 100. Jäger-Division (from Serbia), the 367. Infanterie-Division (from Hungary) and the schwere Panzer-Abteilung 506 (with 45 new Tiger tanks).

German soldiers from the 1. Infanterie-Division pass an abandoned ISU-152 in a snowstorm. Note the soldier carrying the Panzerfaust. (Author)

Note: gridlines are shown at intervals of 5km (3.1miles).

GERMAN UNITS

A. SS-Panzer-Aufklärungs-Abteilung 10 (SS-*Frundsberg*)
B. I./SS-Panzergrenadier-Regiment 21 and II./SS-Panzer-Regiment 10 (SS-*Frundsberg*)
C. Kampfgruppe Stahl/Panzergrenadier-Regiment 114 (6. Panzer-Division)
D. 6./SS-Panzer-Regiment 10 (SS-*Frundsberg*)
E. SS-Panzergrenadier-Regiment 22 (deployed 8 April)
F. SS-Panzergrenadier-Regiment 21 (deployed 9 April)

SS-*Frundsberg*

VON TREUENFELD

6

VON WALDENFELS

GOLGOC
SHVEYKOV
KOVALO
MONASTYRYS'KA
ZAVALE
KOROPETS
DNIESTER RIVER
SOKOLIV
POTOK

▼ **EVENTS**

1. 5 April, 1215hrs: The SS-*Frundsberg* Division begins its attack, with its reconnaissance battalion advancing south-east, bypassing enemy resistance. An intact bridge over the Strypa is captured at Osovtsy (Osowce) by 2100hrs.

2. 6 April, morning: Kampfgruppe Stahl from the 6. Panzer-Division heads north from Yaslovets/Ripynsti and encounters an enemy anti-tank roadblock at Tribukhovtsy.

3. 6 April, morning: The vanguard of SS-*Frundsberg* Division (I./SS-Pz.Gren.Regt. 21 and II./SS-Pz.Regt. 10) encounters strong enemy resistance north of Monastyrys'ka and halts.

4. Stahl sends two Panzergrenadier companies across the Strypa by rubber boat and they advance into the southern edge of Buchach. By 1100hrs, the Soviet blocking detachment withdraws, leaving the town and the bridge in German hands.

5. Afternoon: The 6./SS-Pz.Regt. 10 bypasses enemy resistance via Olesha and approaches the north-west corner of Buchach.

6. 1715hrs: Direct contact is established between the SS-*Frundsberg* tank company and Kampfgruppe Stahl.

7. 1900hrs: Soviet counterattack by the 4GTC recaptures the bridgehead at Osovtsy.

8. 7 April: The SS-*Frundsberg* Division secures Monastyrys'ka with close air support from Ju 87 Stukas from SG 77.

9. The 6./SS-Pz.Regt. 10 attacks to clear Soviet rearguards from the north-east outskirts of Buchach, but one PzKpfw IV tank is knocked out by an anti-tank gun.

10. 8 April: The SS-Pz.Gren.Regt. 22 attacks to the north-east, pushing back Soviet units north-east of Buchach.

11. 10 April: The SS-*Frundsberg* Division conducts an attack with both regiments on line; the SS-Pz.Gren.Regt. 22 is repulsed at Hill 392 but the SS-Pz.Gren.Regt. 21 manages to capture Pilava and Hill 366. Two PzKpfw IV tanks are destroyed by anti-tank guns, while four T-34 tanks are knocked out.

LINK-UP AT BUCHACH, 5–10 APRIL 1944

The climax of the Kamenets-Podolsky campaign occurred at the heretofore obscure Ukrainian village of Buchach on the Strypa River. The link-up of the 6. Panzer-Division and the SS-*Frundsberg* Division opened a tenuous escape corridor for Hube's encircled 1. Panzerarmee to avoid annihilation and the collapse of the German defensive front in Galicia.

PODHAJCE (PODGAYTSY)

1

2

KUYDANOV

OSOVTSY

4

7

ESHA

PEREVOLOKA

5

HILL 392

5

11

E

10

BUCHACH

PILAVA

F

6

HILL 366

6

CASTLE

HILL 374

MEDVEDOVTSY

9

1

TRIBUKHOVTSY

1

4

RIPYNSTI

DZHURYN

2

YASLOVETS

74 XXX ⊠

SHEVERDIN

18 Gd XXX ⊠

AFONIN

SOVIET UNITS
1. Elements of the 155th Rifle Division (74th Rifle Corps)
2. Elements of the 226th Rifle Division (18 GRC)
3. Elements of the 280th Rifle Division (18 GRC)
4. Elements of the 4th Guards Tank Corps
5. Elements of the 8th Rifle Division (deployed 8–9 April)
6. Elements of the 147th Rifle Division (deployed 8–9 April)
7. Elements of the 280th Rifle Division (deployed 8–9 April)
8. Elements of the 226th Rifle Division (deployed 8–9 April)
9. Elements of the 276th Rifle Division (deployed 8–9 April)
10. Elements of the 183rd Rifle Division (deployed 8–9 April)

German troops move on foot through a snow shower. Most of Hube's army conducted the breakout on foot, since operational vehicles were in the spearhead. Note that most of the troops are armed and all seem relatively well equipped for the weather. (Author)

Since it would take four to five days for Hausser's II SS-Panzerkorps to assemble near Lvov and move to the front, on 3 April, Raus ordered the two fresh infantry divisions (100J, 367) to advance and secure the area between the towns of Rohatyn and Berezhany. Raus wanted to use this sector as a forward assembly area for Hausser's II SS-Panzerkorps; from this position the SS-Panzertruppen could move 46km east to relieve the encircled garrison in Tarnopol or 50km south-east to the link-up point at Buchach on the Strypa River. By 4 April, the Rohatyn–Berezhany sector had been occupied without difficulty, primarily because Cherniakhovsky's 60th Army was focused on reducing Tarnopol. Once the assembly area was secure, the reconnaissance battalion from the SS-*Frundsberg* Division moved forward by train to Zloczow, 36km north of Berezhany; it was soon followed by a battalion of PzKpfw IV tanks (II./SS-Pz.Regt. 10) and the SS-Panzergrenadier-Regiment 21. After assembling, these forces began advancing south to secure the vital crossroads town of Podhajce (Podgaytsy). SS-Gruppenführer Karl Fischer von Treuenfeld, the division commander, was an old-school Nazi who had first met Hitler during the 1923 Beer Hall Putsch. During Operation *Barbarossa*, his SS-Brigade had been heavily involved in the liquidation of civilians and rear area security missions. Despite his lack of actual front-line combat experience, the 59-year-old von Treuenfeld was given command of the SS-*Frundsberg* in late 1943 and this campaign was to be his baptism of fire against armed opponents. Zhukov had sent Generalmajor Ivan M. Afonin's 18th Guards Rifle Corps (226, 280RD) to create a screen line between Podhajce and the Dniester River, a distance of 35km, but clearly not intended to stop a mechanized attack. Unable to hold Podhajce, Afonin created a number of entrenched roadblocks to delay the advance of the SS-*Frundsberg* Division. On the afternoon of 5 April, von Treuenfeld began advancing toward Kovalovka, just 16km from Buchach, but was slowed by mud, enemy anti-tank ambushes and occasional mine obstacles. Nevertheless, von Treuenfeld informed Hausser, who then notified Hube by radio that the SS-*Frundsberg* would link up with Korpsgruppe Chevallerie at Buchach the next day.

Meanwhile, the plight of the encircled German garrison in Tarnopol had significant bearing on the actions of both sides. Gruppe Neindorff had been encircled for nearly two weeks by the 60th Army and was being battered by daily attacks, artillery bombardments and bombing. On 25 March, Raus had attempted a relief effort with Kampfgruppe Friebe from the

8. Panzer-Division, but it was unable to fight its way through to Tarnopol. On 31 March, the 60th Army launched a powerful concentric attack with three rifle divisions, which inflicted heavy casualties on the garrison and forced the survivors back into the city centre. On 2 April, Model took over as commander of the Heeresgruppe Nordukraine and he was particularly keen on preventing the annihilation of Gruppe Neindorff, which he thought would seriously degrade front-line morale. Although Hitler refused to countenance evacuating Tarnopol, he did agree to Model's recommendation to use part of Hausser's II SS-Panzerkorps to attempt another relief effort for Tarnopol, even though this would serve as a distraction to the primary goal of re-establishing a ground link with Hube's encircled army. Consequently, Hausser had to prepare for two diverging lines of operations, one to the north-east to Tarnopol (with the SS-*Hohenstaufen* Division) and one to the south-east to Buchach (with the SS-*Frundsberg* Division). Instead of massing this elite formation to accomplish one mission, it would be split into two sub-components which might not be strong enough to accomplish either mission.

During the night of 5/6 April, Major Paul Stahl's Kampfgruppe (with a total strength of fewer than 700 troops) reached the village of Ripynsti and discovered a strong Soviet blocking position in the village of Tribukhovtsy, 4.5km east of Buchach. The blocking detachment included infantry from the 74th Rifle Corps, reinforced with some tanks from the 14th Guards Tank Brigade (4GTC). Stahl decided to send two Panzergrenadier companies across the Strypa River by rubber boat, while the rest of his command began probing the Soviet blocking position at first light on 6 April. Although the Soviets conducted a tenacious defence at Tribukhovtsy, as soon as they learned that German infantry was advancing into Buchach from the south-west, they began to evacuate. By 1100hrs, most of Buchach was occupied by Stahl's troops after brief house-to-house fighting, but only 20 prisoners were taken in the town. Not only had the retreating Soviet troops abandoned two SU-76 assault guns and a number of 45mm anti-tank guns, but they had also failed to destroy the small road bridge at Buchach, which was now the primary escape path for Hube's army. While exuberant about capturing this critical objective, Stahl was chagrined to find that no relief force was in sight – as expected. Where was the II SS-Panzerkorps?

While Stahl had been desperately fighting his way into Buchach, the SS-*Frundsberg* Division had been moving slowly and with little sense of urgency. Von Treuenfeld sent most of his reconnaissance battalion toward the south-east, while his advance guard (the I./SS-Panzergrenadier-Regiment 21 and SS-Hauptscharführer Leo Franke's 6./SS-Pz.Regt. 10) took a diverging path due south. Moving cautiously, the SS tankers and Panzergrenadiers encountered elements of Afonin's 18GRC holding a series of fortified villages north of the crossroads town of Monastyrys'ka (15km west of Buchach). Although lightly armed, Afonin's veteran troops inflicted significant casualties upon the road-bound SS-Panzergrenadiers with mortars and harassing flank attacks; Franke was among those wounded. It is important to note that Hausser had been told by Hitler to avoid suffering unnecessary casualties so that the II SS-Panzerkorps could be returned intact to France, which had undoubtedly been passed on to von Treuenfeld. Uncertain about attacking a strong enemy force in Monastyrys'ka with just two battalions, von Treuenfeld decided to bring up his artillery and more infantry, which consumed much of the day. By late afternoon, it was apparent that the SS-*Frundsberg* Division

LUFTWAFFE LIAISON TEAM COORDINATES AIR DROP FOR THE 6. PANZER-DIVISION, 5 APRIL 1944 (PP. 78–79)

The Wehrmacht had learned a great deal from efforts to supply previous encircled units by air in 1942–43 and soon after Hube's army was cut off, Luftflotte 4 organized three four-man air liaison teams and flew them into the pocket. Unlike previous airlifts that relied upon deliveries to fixed airfields, Hube's 'wandering *Kessel*' was on the move and aerial supply needed to move with it. The Luftwaffe teams were responsible for setting up radio beacons to mark new drop zones for aerial resupply missions and to assist forward combat units with requesting emergency air drops of fuel and ammunition.

On 5 April, a Kampfgruppe from the 6. Panzer-Division, led by Major Paul Stahl, had reached the village of Yaslovets, just 12km from the expected link-up with the 4. Panzerarmee relief force at

Buchach. However, Stahl's tanks and half-tracks **(1)** were nearly out of fuel and he directed the attached Luftwaffe liaison team to request an airdrop of fuel. The Luftwaffe team used a Torn.Fu d2 tactical radio **(2)** to request a daylight airdrop, then fired flares **(2B)** to mark the drop zone when several Ju 52 transports arrived later that afternoon. Each Ju 52 **(3)** dropped six to eight supply cannisters (*Abwurfbehälter für Nachschub*) by parachute **(4)**. A cannister could hold up to 460 litres of fuel, so two were needed just to refill one Panther tank. Only enough fuel was delivered to enable the Kampfgruppe to reach the next objective, but it was critical for mission success. With this additional fuel, Major Stahl's Kampfgruppe was able to reach Buchach the next day and achieve a tenuous link with the lead elements of the SS-*Frundsberg* Division.

could not eliminate this enemy blocking position and reach Buchach before sunset, so it was time to rethink the problem. Apparently, one of the Panzergrenadier commanders recommended using the tank company (now under SS-Untersturmführer Hans Quandel) to bypass the roadblock and reach Buchach before sunset, so that they could report mission success. Von Treuenfeld not only agreed but decided to accompany Quandel's 14 PzKpfw IV tanks, while his vanguard remained immobilized outside Monastyrys'ka. After a roundabout journey of about 20km, the column approached the outskirts of Buchach around 1700hrs, without encountering any resistance along the way. Just outside the town, von Treuenfeld's SPW was disabled by a mine, but Quandel's tanks continued, and around 1715hrs met Stahl's Panzergrenadiers. The first tentative contact between the 4. Panzerarmee and Hube's encircled army had been established. Von Treuenfeld sent a quick radio report to Raus, simply stating, 'Contact re-established.'

In fact, Hube's army still had a long way to go until it escaped from Zhukov's encirclement. The SS-*Frundsberg*'s movement to Buchach was little more than a company-size raid, and von Treuenfeld did not send any Panzergrenadiers to help hold the town for another 24 hours. Indeed, aside from Quandel's Panzers, the SS-*Frundsberg* did not even hold the road open back to Monastyrys'ka, which Afonin's troops could still interdict. Stahl was informed that he was responsible for holding the Buchach corridor open with his two exhausted Panzergrenadier battalions, which were reduced to just 177 effectives, supported by two Panthers under Major Karl von Sivers. Nor would the SS-*Hohenstaufen* be any help, since it was entirely focused on getting ready to mount another relief operation toward Tarnopol. On the east side

An SU-85 assault gun approaches the Panther it knocked out. The Panther was surprisingly vulnerable to flank shots against its thinner armour, which could ignite its fuel cells. (Author)

Abandoned Wespe self-propelled 10.5cm howitzers. Although the 1. Panzerarmee lost a large portion of its artillery in the retreat, about one-third of the self-propelled Wespe and Hummel pieces made it across the Strypa River. (Author)

of the Strypa, the 6. Panzer-Division now had to hold the escape corridor open and the lengthy road leading to it, for the rest of Hube's 1. Panzerarmee to retreat along. Instead of a firm, corps-size handshake at Buchach, Hube's vanguard encountered only a tentative fist-bump that was not resourced to hold open a mobility corridor adequate for a 200,000-man army to move through. Hube was also disappointed to learn that the huge supply convoy promised by the OKH was 50km back near Berezhany and that 1. Panzerarmee would need to advance well past the Strypa before it could be resupplied.

From Zhukov's perspective, Hube's army could still be crushed, although it was proving more difficult to accomplish than he expected. He continued to transfer units – mostly depleted from heavy losses – to try and block Hube's escape route. There were elements of five Soviet rifle divisions in the vicinity of Buchach, but very little armour. The 8GMC from Katukov's 1TA was 40km to the south-west near Stanislav, but on the wrong side of the Dniester River and fully engaged against the Hungarian VII Army Corps. Katukov's other corps, the 11GTC, tried to recross the Dniester at Ustechko but unexpectedly bumped into the 17. Panzer-Division and lost 35 AFVs. Poluboyarov's 4th Guards Tank Corps were about 30km north of Buchach, but this formation was fully committed to opposing German attempts to relieve the isolated Tarnopol garrison. Nevertheless, Zhukov ordered the 4GTC to send two of its brigades to Trembovla (Terebovlya) to assemble for a counterattack toward Buchach. He also ordered Generalmajor Vasily E. Grigoriev's 31st Tank Corps, which had been detached from Katukov's 1TA since late February in order to reconstitute in reserve, to send a battlegroup to reinforce Soviet infantry units in the Buchach sector. Grigoriev still only had small numbers of AFVs and anti-tank guns, but he sent them forward as ordered. Even with these stopgap measures, Zhukov had no substantial armoured force to hurl against the narrow escape corridor at the Buchach bridgehead. The Soviet pursuit of Hube's withdrawing army, primarily led by Grechko's 1GA and Moskalenko's 38th Army, had also slowed to a walking pace; Moskalenko's army had been stripped of all its armour and about half its infantry. Indeed, both Hube and Zhukov were in a similar predicament, with intermixed, badly depleted and poorly supplied units that were just about fought out.

On 7 April, Hube pulled his last units across the Seret River and formed a thin defensive front facing eastward to delay the Soviet pursuit. At the same time, Korpsgruppe Chevallerie and the SS-*Frundsberg* Division began a series of local attacks to expand the narrow

corridor at Buchach. The 367. Infanterie-Division, one of the units transferred from occupation duty in Budapest, was brought forward to occupy the area south of the town down to the Dniester River. Likewise, the 100. Jäger-Division was assigned to clear out the area north of Buchach. The fight to expand the corridor would continue for several days and the Germans had the advantage that at least some of their units were fresh and nearly full-strength. The SS-*Frundsberg* Division launched a two-battalion attack on the morning of 8 April, which cleared the last Soviet defenders out of the northern suburbs of Buchach. That afternoon, Generalfeldmarschall Model came forward to Buchach to meet Hube at the command post of the 6. Panzer-Division. Model knew Hube well, since they had been classmates at the gymnasium in Naumburg over 30 years before. Model told Hube that he wanted 1. PzAOK to form a defensive front along the Seret River, stretching 40km from Chortkov to the Dniester River, and to 'hold it at all cost'. Hube warned that his exhausted army could hold on the Seret only for a few days at best and the corridor at Buchach was still highly vulnerable, but he complied and issued an order for a defence of the Seret River at 1430hrs.

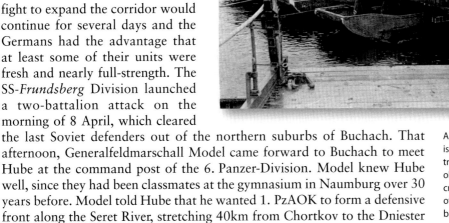

A section of pontoon bridge is used to ferry German troops across a minor water obstacle. Hube's army had to cross numerous tributaries of the Dniester River with a bare minimum of engineering support. (Nik Cornish at www.stavka.photos)

Model was less concerned about Buchach or the poor condition of Hube's army than he was about Soviet activities at Tarnopol and south of the city. German intelligence spotted the modest assembly of Soviet armour from 4GTC and 31TC near Trembovla on the Seret, midway between Tarnopol and Buchach, but incorrectly assessed it as two full-strength tank corps. Anticipating another large-scale Soviet armoured attack, Model preferred to use Hausser's II SS-Panzerkorps to conduct a spoiling attack at Trembovla and relieve Tarnopol. He judged that Hube's army was not in immediate danger and decided to pull most of the SS-*Frundsberg* Division out of the Buchach sector and move it north to deal with the Soviet armour at Trembovla. However, Hube did not see the situation that way and went over Model's head to make a direct appeal to Hitler for permission to withdraw his battered army back behind the Strypa River. Amazingly, on the night of 9 April, Hitler agreed to Hube's request but also stipulated that Model would continue with the operation to relieve Tarnopol.

Even though Hausser's II SS-Panzerkorps had opened up a line of communications to the lead elements of Korpsgruppe Chevallerie, this afforded little sustenance to Hube's army. On 9 April, a small column with 100 tons of rations and 200 tons of 10.5cm howitzer ammunition made it through Buchach to the east, but the corridor was still under enemy artillery fire. Thus, the next day the SS-*Frundsberg* Division conducted another attack with both its regiments, which further expanded the corridor and pushed back some of the enemy artillery. On the morning of 11 April, Hube's 1. Panzerarmee began marching west, toward the Buchach corridor. Hube's

A StuG III Ausf G rolls through a Ukrainian village. The turretless assault gun was intended for defence and proved ill-suited to movement-to-contact missions that were the staple of the breakout. (Fotoarchiv für Zeitgeschichte/Archiv/Süddeutsche Zeitung Photo)

A Soviet T-34 Model 1943 tank from Rybalko's 3GTA burns near the town of Buchach, April 1944. Except for the initial breakthrough attacks, the 1st Ukrainian Front's armour was dispersed throughout most of the campaign and could not employ any real mass against Hube's breakout operation. (Author)

intent was to create a *Rollbahn* along the Chortkov–Buchach road, but the Soviets had deployed two brigade-size blocking positions around Dzuhryn that required 24 hours to eliminate. After that, the way was relatively clear and Hube was able to establish flank guards, which protected the main body from enemy interference as it headed westward. As it became increasingly clear that the 1. Panzerarmee was escaping to the west, the recriminations began on the Soviet side. On 12 April, a Soviet intelligence officer in the 237th Rifle Division, Major Konstantin I. Andreev, apparently delivered a situation update to the corps commander, Generalmajor Ivan M. Afonin, which did not go down well. Afonin, a protégé of Zhukov since the Battle of Khalkhin-Gol in 1939, personally shot and killed the major after a heated exchange. Even by Red Army standards, 'shooting the messenger of bad news' was an unusual event and the army commander Cherniakhovsky reported it to the Central Committee. However, Zhukov quashed the investigation and made sure that Afonin received a Hero of the Soviet Union (HSU) award for his efforts in the campaign.

Meanwhile, Model began a major relief operation toward Tarnopol, utilizing over 90 AFVs from the SS-*Hohenstaufen* Division, Kampfgruppe Friebe and the s.Pz.Abt. 507. Zhukov ensured that Cherniakhovsky's 60th Army had plenty of artillery and anti-tank guns to blunt the German armoured spearhead, which managed to advance only a few kilometres toward its objective. Heavy rains on 12 April halted the German attack, which was not resumed until 15 April. Model made a desperate, costly lunge with his best units, but was stopped 8km short of Tarnopol. The Soviets accelerated their attacks on the encircled German garrison and Generalmajor von Neindorff was killed by enemy artillery fire. On the night of 16/17 April, the survivors in the garrison attempted a breakout, but only 55 men were able to reach German lines. Thereafter, the Soviets occupied the devastated ruins of Tarnopol and the German relief forces pulled back to their original start line. The SS-*Hohenstaufen* Division suffered considerable casualties in the futile Tarnopol relief operation, for no tactical gain.

The only real value of the Tarnopol relief operation was that it distracted Soviet attention away from the Buchach corridor for nearly a week, while Hube's army was escaping over the Strypa River. The Soviet armoured concentration at Trembovla that concerned Model so much proved unable to launch any serious counterattack. By 20 April, the last elements of the 1. PzAOK had crossed over the Strypa and Hube's forces had accomplished the largest breakout operation in military history. An encircled force of over 200,000 troops had moved 90–100km through enemy-held territory under adverse weather conditions and with minimal supplies. In contrast, during the 1950 Battle of the Chosin Reservoir in the Korean War, about 30,000 troops in the US X Corps conducted a 70km breakout through enemy lines in the midst of severe weather conditions. After the conclusion of

Although Hube's 1. Panzerarmee conducted a successful breakout, it was forced to abandon most of its heavy weapons and vehicles for lack of sufficient fuel and spare parts. These losses would never be made good. Here an sFH 18 howitzer and multiple trucks litter the frozen battlefield. (Author)

the Kamenets-Podolsky campaign, both Zhukov's 1st Ukrainian Front and Model's Heeresgruppe Nordukraine were totally exhausted, and a relative lull settled over the area for the next three months until the Lvov–Sandomierz offensive began. Although Zhukov had achieved a major operational victory in the Proskurov–Chernovtsy operation, particularly in terms of territorial objectives, he did not get the battle of annihilation that had been his primary campaign objective. Indeed, the escape of Hube's army from encirclement – coming so soon after the partly successful German breakout from the Korsun Pocket – was embarrassing to Zhukov. In his post-war memoirs, Zhukov claimed that the 1. Panzerarmee lost more than half its personnel in the campaign (i.e., over 100,000 troops) and virtually all its equipment. Due to Hube's successful breakout and Zhukov's self-exonerating claims, Soviet historiography tended to minimize the Kamenets-Podolsky campaign.

Survivors of Hube's 1. Panzerarmee mounted on Russian ponies. These were likely artillerymen or support troops, who had more access to horses than the infantrymen, who walked out of the pocket. Note the bare minimum of field kit. (Author)

AFTERMATH

On the day that the last of his army crossed the Strypa River and was reintegrated into the main German defensive front, Hube flew back to Berchtesgaden to meet with Hitler, who was celebrating his birthday. Although normally averse to endorsing retreats, Hitler recognized the escape of the 1. Panzerarmee as a great feat of arms and was impressed with Hube's never-say-die leadership ethos. Thus, Hitler gratefully awarded Hube with the Diamonds to his *Ritterkreuz des Eisernen Kreuzes* (Knight's Cross of the Iron Cross) and promoted him to Generaloberst. Hitler was impressed with Hube's fighting spirit and wanted leaders like this to direct the increasingly dire situation on the Eastern Front, but it is unclear what role Hube might have played after Kamenets-Podolsky. Certainly, he would have been considered for an army group command. However, when flying back to the Eastern Front on 21 April, Hube's He 111 clipped a tree upon take-off from Berchtesgaden and he was killed in the ensuing crash. Von der Chevallerie took over temporary command of the 1. Panzerarmee, which would continue to fight on the Eastern Front until the end of the war. Five days after the 1. Panzerarmee finished crossing the Strypa River, Hausser's II SS-Panzerkorps was pulled out of the line and placed into reserve near Lvov.

Soviet sources claim that during the Proskurov–Chernovtsy operation, the 1st Ukrainian Front captured 849 tanks and self-propelled guns, 406

A Tiger from the s.Pz.Abt. 506, which was attached to the 100. Jäger-Division in early April 1944. During 6–9 April, the battalion destroyed over 30 T-34 tanks, at no loss to itself. Note the Soviet truck with 76.2mm gun burning in the background. (Author)

The final evacuation of the 1. Panzerarmee, 7–20 April 1944

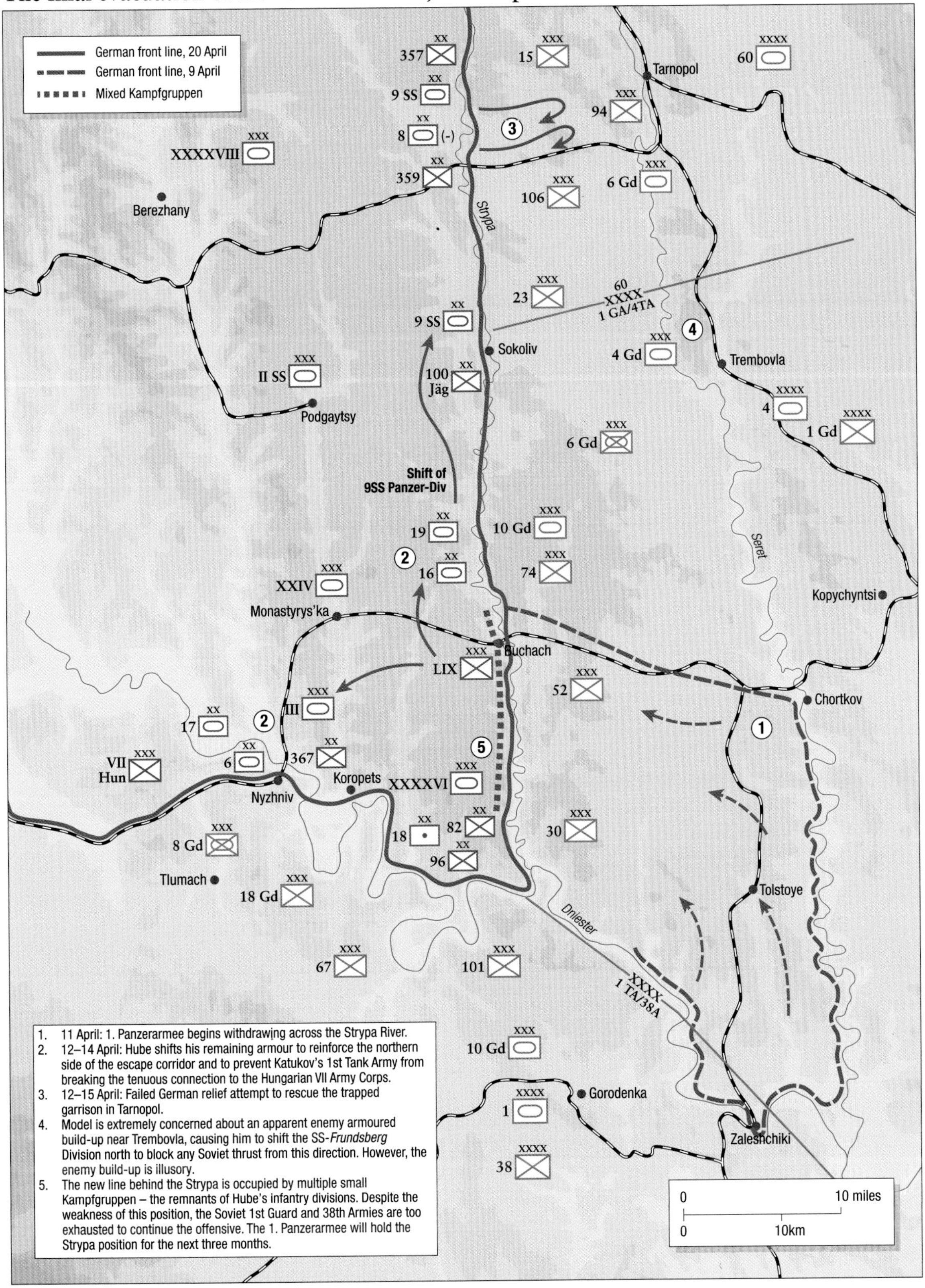

Legend:
- German front line, 20 April
- German front line, 9 April
- Mixed Kampfgruppen

Map labels:

357, XX
15, XXX
Tarnopol
60, XXXX
9 SS, XX
94, XXX
8, XX (-)
3
XXXXVIII, XXX
359, XX
106, XXX
6 Gd, XXX
Berezhany
Strypa
23, XXX
60 XXXX 1 GA/4TA
4
9 SS, XX
Sokoliv
4 Gd, XXX
Trembovla
II SS, XXX
100 Jäg, XX
4, XXXX
Podgaytsy
6 Gd, XXX
1 Gd, XXXX
Seret
Shift of 9SS Panzer-Div
19, XX
10 Gd, XXX
2
16, XX
74, XXX
XXIV, XXX
Monastyrys'ka
Kopychyntsi
LIX, XXX
Buchach
52, XXX
Chortkov
17, XX
2
III, XXX
1
VII Hun, XXX
6, XX
367, XX
5
XXXXVI, XXX
Koropets
Nyzhniv
8 Gd, XXX
18, XX
82, XX
30, XXX
96, XX
Tlumach
18 Gd, XXX
Tolstoye
Dniester
XXXX 1 TA/38A
67, XXX
101, XXX
10 Gd, XXX
1, XXXX
Gorodenka
38, XXXX
Zaleshchiki

1. 11 April: 1. Panzerarmee begins withdrawing across the Strypa River.
2. 12–14 April: Hube shifts his remaining armour to reinforce the northern side of the escape corridor and to prevent Katukov's 1st Tank Army from breaking the tenuous connection to the Hungarian VII Army Corps.
3. 12–15 April: Failed German relief attempt to rescue the trapped garrison in Tarnopol.
4. Model is extremely concerned about an apparent enemy armoured build-up near Trembovla, causing him to shift the SS-*Frundsberg* Division north to block any Soviet thrust from this direction. However, the enemy build-up is illusory.
5. The new line behind the Strypa is occupied by multiple small Kampfgruppen – the remnants of Hube's infantry divisions. Despite the weakness of this position, the Soviet 1st Guard and 38th Armies are too exhausted to continue the offensive. The 1. Panzerarmee will hold the Strypa position for the next three months.

0 ____ 10 miles
0 ____ 10km

armoured personnel carriers (SPW), 2,086 guns of various calibres, 31,468 motor vehicles and a large amount of other military materiel. In addition, the Soviets claim to have captured 24,950 German soldiers. More recent Russian sources modified these claims to 322 tanks, 39 assault guns, 64 tank destroyers, 79 self-propelled artillery and 21,959 motor vehicles. Of note, at the start of the campaign, the 1. PzAOK had about 850 tanks and assault guns, of which only about one-third were operational. Most of the vehicles lost in the retreat were either out of fuel or non-operational and blown up to prevent capture. On 7 April 1944, Korpsgruppe Breith conducted a survey of remaining manpower and equipment in its formations, and reported the following (personnel strength in parentheses):

- 6. and 11. Panzer-Divisionen: Pz.Gren.Regt. 4 (380), Pz.Gren.Regt. 114 (450), Pz.Gren.Regt. 110 (120); 2 Panthers, 6 Hornisse, 3 Marder III; 15 artillery pieces (incl. 3 Hummel)
- 17. Panzer-Division: II./Pz.Gren.Regt. 40 (130), II./Pz.Gren.Regt. 63 (112); Pz.Aufkl.Abt. 117 (140); 1 Tiger, 7 Panther, 6 PzKpfw IV, 13 StuG III, 7 Marder III; 33 artillery pieces (incl. 4 Wespe and 6 Hummel) and 13 7.5cm Pak guns
- 1. Infanterie-Division: combat strength (1,411); 6 artillery pieces, no anti-tank guns
- 75. Infanterie-Division: combat strength (1,922); 8 artillery pieces and one 7.5cm Pak gun
- 82. Infanterie-Division: combat strength (809); 6 artillery pieces, no anti-tank guns
- 101. Jäger-Division: no report received
- 168. Infanterie-Division: combat strength (1,100), plus 200 survivors from SS-*Reich*; 2 Marder III; 25 artillery pieces and 7 7.5cm Pak guns
- 254. Infanterie-Division: Gren.Regt. 454 (398), Gren.Regt. 484 (432); 8 artillery pieces
- 18. Artillerie-Division: Werfer Regt. 1 (392), Artillerie-Regiment 288 (926); 2 StuG III; 16 artillery pieces (incl. 4 Wespe, 2 Hummel)
- Altogether: about 9,500 troops, 16 tanks, 15 assault guns, 18 tank destroyers, 109 artillery pieces (incl. 8 Wespe and 11 Hummel) and 21 towed anti-tank guns

Less data is available from Korpsgruppe Chevallerie, but it is clear that the 1. Panzerarmee was left with very little infantry, about 100 AFVs (roughly 35 tanks, 40 assault guns and 25 tank destroyers), 200+ artillery pieces and perhaps 50 anti-tank guns. Losses in motor transport were horrific, with Kampfgruppe Stahl, one of the strongest groups, reaching the Strypa River with a total of only one SPW, 25 trucks, six RSO tractors and seven Kubelwagen (just 13 per cent of its authorized vehicle strength). While none of Hube's divisions was destroyed, all were reduced to scarecrows with minimal heavy equipment and vehicles remaining. Six of the ten Panzer-Divisionen (6, 11, 19, 25, SS-*Das Reich* and SS-*LSSAH*) that escaped from the *Kessel* had to be sent to the West to refit, and the four that remained on the Ostfront spent months rebuilding and were still not fully restored for the summer campaign. In terms of human casualties, German records, although incomplete for 1. PzAOK during the time it was encircled, suggest that Hube's army suffered a total of 21,300 casualties from 10 March to 10 April, including an

German Waffen-SS infantry from II SS-Panzerkorps move through a shattered town, probably during the effort to relieve the encircled garrison in Tarnopol. (Scherl/Süddeutsche Zeitung Photo)

estimated 3,400 dead, 13,900 wounded and 4,000 missing. When casualties from the first week of Zhukov's offensive are included, Hube's losses rise to a total of about 22,000 or 10 per cent of his starting strength. Raus' 4. PzAOK suffered another 15,000 casualties during the campaign, but not all of which occurred in the primary Tarnopol–Proskurov sector. Soviet sources claim that the 1. Panzerarmee and the II SS-Panzerkorps relief force suffered about 80,000 casualties, including 25,000 captured, which is similar to earlier exaggerations about German losses in the Korsun Pocket. In fact, Hausser's II SS-Panzerkorps suffered only 3,087 casualties and the Tarnopol garrison lost over 4,000 troops, so it would be fair to say that the Kamenets-Podolsky campaign cost the Wehrmacht at least 40,000 casualties, of whom 15,000 were dead or missing. Hube's army had been badly battered, losing roughly 80 per cent of its equipment, but 80 per cent of its troops had escaped to fight another day – which Soviet propaganda would not admit.

Luftflotte 4 flew about 8,000 sorties to support Hube's encircled army, delivering an estimated 3,500–4,000 tons of supplies. Although the Luftwaffe never came close to meeting 1. PzAOK's daily supply requirements, the amount of ammunition and fuel delivered was just enough to keep the spearhead units moving west. Compared to earlier airlift operations, Luftflotte 4's losses during the Kamenets-Podolsky were relatively light, with only about 11 Ju 52s lost to enemy action and nine more to non-battle causes (about 8 per cent of the transports committed to the operation). Luftwaffe transport losses were low because most missions were flown at night and the Soviet VVS had virtually no ability to conduct intercepts under these conditions. In contrast, Luftflotte 4 lost roughly 60 combat aircraft to enemy action, more than half being ground attack aircraft. Nevertheless, the failure of the 2VA to make a greater effort to interdict the lifeline that had been thrown to Hube's army had a great impact upon the course of the campaign.

Zhukov's 1st Ukrainian Front suffered 220,000 casualties (including 60,000 dead or missing) during the Proskurov–Chernovtsy operation, or roughly 25 per cent of its starting strength. According to one Russian source,

Soviet armour losses in the operation amounted to 551 tanks and 134 self-propelled guns, or roughly 48 per cent of the starting operational strength of AFVs. More to the point, all three of Zhukov's tank armies were so depleted at the conclusion of the operation that they would require at least two months to refit and replace their losses; both the 3GTA and 4TA were *hors de combat*. It is true that Zhukov had succeeded in removing a great deal of the Ostheer's armoured strength from the battlefield, but it came at the cost of temporarily sidelining three of the six Soviet tank armies. In the long run, Zhukov had two key advantages in his favour: the Red Army was more capable of replacing its human and materiel losses than the Ostheer, and by the time that the 1st Ukrainian Front resumed its offensive in the summer, the Wehrmacht would no longer be able to transfer major reinforcements from the West to regain the local initiative.

ANALYSIS

Hube managed to conduct a successful breakout attack, even with his depleted forces, primarily due to three reasons. First, Hube achieved operational-level surprise by advancing west instead of south; to be fair, the western line of operations was von Manstein's idea, but it was up to Hube to pull it off. Second, Hube's breakout plan was simple and focused on a clear objective to reach the Strypa River. He also ensured that all subordinate commanders and subunits understood the commander's intent and were focused on that objective. Third, Hube employed his best remaining forces in order to achieve mass at the critical points on the battlefield. Hube's task organization ensured that he had maximum combat power at the tip of the spear, and that these vanguard units did not run out of ammunition or fuel. Tactically, the 1. Panzerarmee used very mixed Kampfgruppen but they did not always have the level of support they were accustomed to, since so much equipment had to be abandoned along the way. Overall, the breakout of the 1. Panzerarmee was a tour de force in operational and tactical-level military leadership, demonstrating what unit cohesion and trained, motivated troops can achieve even when operating under the most adverse battlefield conditions.

In contrast, Zhukov underperformed throughout the campaign because he failed to realistically consider possible enemy courses of action and tried to conduct massive manoeuvre operations on a logistic shoestring. Due to his logistical shortfalls, Zhukov was forced to conduct the operation in two distinct 'pulses', with the first beginning on 5 March and the second on 21 March. Both offensive pulses achieved impressive advances at first, but then quickly began to run out of steam after four to five days. Zhukov did not anticipate Balck's counteroffensive which halted his first offensive pulse, nor the actions of Gruppe Mauss which got in the way of his second offensive pulse. Zhukov used manoeuvre to gain ground, but he failed to fully encircle isolated German units, thereby allowing them to escape. At the decisive moment in the campaign, Zhukov was caught off guard because he was convinced that Hube would attempt to retreat to the south and did not immediately accept when his judgement proved incorrect. Rather than ensuring that his subordinate commanders were focused on cornering and annihilating Hube's army, Zhukov encouraged his subordinates to pursue competing priorities; Katukov was focused on crushing the Hungarian VII

Army Corps while Cherniakhovsky was focused on crushing the German garrison in Tarnopol. Coordination between the other armies arrayed against the 1. Panzerarmee became increasingly disjointed. The fact that Zhukov allowed his remaining armour to become so dispersed and opted not to maintain any significant operational-level reserves to deal with contingencies were serious errors. The escape of Hube's 1. Panzerarmee had far-reaching strategic consequences because it delayed a collapse of the German position on the Eastern Front by at least three months. Had Zhukov succeeded in crushing Hube's army, the *Ostheer*'s entire southern wing would likely have collapsed more quickly, enabling the Red Army to advance into Poland and the Balkans prior to the Allied landing in France. A more rapid German defeat in the East in 1944 would likely have enabled the Red Army to advance farther west into central Europe before the Allies could reach the Rhine.

The 1944 Kamenets-Podolsky campaign also serves to illustrate important lessons for modern military leaders about the use of intelligence in making critical decisions on the battlefield. The Red Army did not endorse alternative analysis and instead intelligence tended to be used to support scripted assessments from front-level commanders, the Stavka and Stalin. Rather than try to use intelligence collection assets (e.g. aerial reconnaissance, radio intercepts) to determine which courses of action the enemy was actually adopting and then making an appropriate counter response, the Red Army tended to act as if it did not really matter which course of action the enemy chose. To be fair, the Wehrmacht of 1944 was often guilty of the same error. Nevertheless, a professional military intelligence assessment should always address the range of possible enemy courses of action, focusing particularly on their most likely course of action and their most dangerous. Had the 1st Ukrainian Front done so, Zhukov would likely have kept a mobile reserve to deal with a possible breakout attempt to the west. A single full-strength tank corps would probably have been sufficient to block Hube's escape route through Buchach until Zhukov could mass his dispersed combat power to immobilize and crush the 1. Panzerarmee. To his credit, Zhukov would learn from his mistakes at Kamenets-Podolsky, and his next round of offensives would prove far more decisive.

German troops survey three knocked-out Soviet T-34 tanks on the outskirts of Tarnopol. The effort to relieve the remaining 1,200-man garrison in Tarnopol proved to be a major distraction for the II SS-Panzerkorps, which was unable to devote its full resources to extracting Hube's 200,000-man army from its encirclement. (Fotoarchiv für Zeitgeschichte/Archiv/Süddeutsche Zeitung Photo)

THE BATTLEFIELD TODAY

During the Soviet era, a number of monuments were built in the western Ukraine to commemorate the 1944 Kamenets-Podolsky campaign. In particular, Vinnitsa, Kamenets-Podolsky, Zhmerynka and Tarnopol had an assortment of monuments, memorials and military cemeteries related to the 1944 campaign. At the time, the Soviet government used these monuments to highlight the role of the Red Army in liberating the western Ukraine. However, since the 2014 Russian seizure of the Crimea and then the 2022 invasion of Ukraine, many Soviet-era monuments in the region have been defaced, removed or otherwise neglected. A new Ukrainian law enacted in 2015 requiring the removal of memorials linked to the communist regime provided a legal imprimatur to the task. Whether or not tourists will find many of these older monuments extant after the conclusion of the current Russo-Ukrainian War is uncertain. For example, a monument to Badanov's 4th Tank Army (with the obligatory T-34 tank on a plinth) in Kamenets-Podolsky was taken down in June 2022, four months after the Russian invasion began. Reminders of the German occupation are even more difficult to find, aside from occasional battlefield salvage items. One exception is a few World War II-era concrete bunkers west of Kamenets-Podolsky, near the Zbruch River. The castle at Kamenets-Podolsky is worth a visit, since it still bears some scars from the 1944 fighting.

Villages like Buchach, 98km west of Kamenets-Podolsky, have changed relatively little since Hube's Panzers achieved their breakout at that point nearly 80 years ago. The Strypa River, like the Seret River, provides little in the way of photo opportunities. There is plenty of history to find in western Ukraine, but most of it takes local guides and an abundance of time. However, given the ongoing war and the general level of destruction across Ukraine, it is likely going to be some time before tourism recovers.

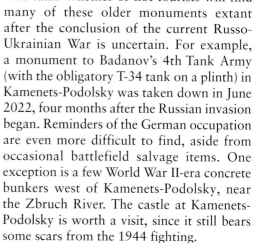

Mass grave of Soviet soldiers in Kamenets-Podolsky prior to 2022. Although many of the Red Army soldiers who liberated this region in 1944 were ethnic Ukrainians, the fate of such Soviet-era memorials is uncertain in light of the current Russo-Ukrainian War, but most will probably be removed. (Author)

Ukrainian workers remove a T-34 tank from Kamenets-Podolsky square in June 2022. Plates listing the names of Soviet soldiers killed in the liberation of the city were also removed. (Author)

In lieu of Soviet-era T-34 tanks, the mayor of Tarnopol (Ternopil) decided to display captured modern Russian tanks in the public square in 2022. (Author)

FURTHER READING

Primary Source Records

Anlage 25, Kriegstagebuch 2, I./Pz.Rgt. 26 (Bundesarchiv-Militärarchiv, RH 39/599)

KTB Nr. 13, 1a, 1. Panzerarmee, 25–31 March 1944 and 1–10 April 1944, National Archives and Research Administration (NARA), T313, Roll 71

Anhang zum KTB Nr. 13 mit Anlagen, 'über Tätigkeit asserhalb des Kessels', vom. 23.3–9.4.1944, National Archives and Research Administration (NARA), T313, Roll 74, Frame 7312784

Kriegstagebuch (KTB), Panzergrenadier-Regiment 1, 8 March to 12 December 1944

KTB, I./Pz.Gren.Regt. 114, 1 January to 15 May 1944, National Archives and Research Administration (NARA), T315, Roll 352, Frame 805.

KTB, Der 6./SS Pz.Regt. 10 – Darstellung der Ereignisse, 2–24 April 1944, National Archives and Research Administration (NARA), T354, Roll 152, Frame 3794562.

KTB, 17. Panzer-Division, February–December 1944, National Archives and Research Administration (NARA), T315, Roll 693.

Gefechtsbericht über das Gefecht bei Sosnowka-Bissowka am 4.3.1944, 6. Panzer-Division, 13 March 1944, National Archives and Research Administration (NARA), T313, Roll 70, F7307229.

Journal of military operations 3rd Guards Tank Army (Журнал боевых действий 3 гв. ТА), 1–31 March 1944, TsAMO, Fund: 315, Inventory: 4,440, File: 334.

Journal of military operations 31st Tank Corps (Журнал боевых действий 31 тк), 23 March to 12 April 1944, TsAMO, Fund: 3,421, Inventory: 1, File: 11.

Combat Log, 38th Army, 15–20 March 1944.

Memoirs

Balck, Hermann, *Order in Chaos: The Memoirs of General of Panzer Troops Hermann Balck*, Lexington: The University Press of Kentucky (2017)

Bessonov, Evgeni, *Tank Rider: Into the Reich with the Red Army*, Philadelphia: Casemate (2005)

Katukov, Mikhail E., *Na ostriye glavnogo udara* [*On the edge of the main blow*], Moscow: Military Publishing House (1974)

Morzik, Fritz, *German Air Force Airlift Operations*, Honolulu: University Press of the Pacific (2002)

Moskalenko, Kirill S., *Na Yugo-Zapadnom Napravlenii, 1943–1945* [*On the South-Western Direction 1943–1945*], Moscow: Nauka (1973)

Schiebel, Helmut, *A Better Comrade You Will Never Find: A Panzerjäger on the Eastern Front 1941–1945*, Winnipeg: J. J. Fedorowicz Publishing Inc. (2010)

Secondary Sources

Buttar, Prit, *The Reckoning: The Defeat of Army Group South, 1944*, Oxford: Osprey Publishing (2020)

Davie, H. G. W., 'Logistics of the Tank Army: The Uman–Botoşani Operation, 1944', *Journal of Slavic Military Studies*, Volume 33, Issue 3 (December 2020), pp. 420–41

'Encirclement of a Panzer Army Near Kamenets-Podolskiy', chapter 6 of *Operations of Encircled Forces: Experiences of German Forces in Russia*, Pamphlet 20–234, Washington, DC: United States Department of the Army (1952)

Glantz, David M., *Atlas of the Proskurov-Chernovitsy Operation, 4 March–17 April 1944*, Self-published (2006)

Hinze, Rolf, *Crucible of Combat: Germany's Defensive Battles in the Ukraine, 1943–44*, Solihull: Helion & Co. Ltd. (2009)

Isaev, Aleksei, *'Kotol' Khube. Proskurovsko-Chernovitskaya Operatsiya 1944 goda* [*Hube's 'cauldron'. Proskurov-Chernivtsi Operation in 1944*], Moscow: Yauza (2017)

Lehmann, Rudolf and Ralf Tiemann, *The Leibstandarte*, vol. IV/1, Winnipeg: J. J. Fedorowicz Publishing Inc. (1993)

Liedtke, Gregory, 'Lost in the Mud: The (Nearly) Forgotten Collapse of the German Army in the Western Ukraine, March and April 1944', *The Journal of Slavic Military Studies*, Vol. 28, Issue No. 1, 2015, pp. 215–38.

Reynolds, Michael, *Sons of the Reich: II SS-Panzerkorps*, Barnsley: Pen & Sword Books (2002)

Stenger, Dieter, *Panzers East and West: The German 10th SS Panzer Division from the Eastern Front to Normandy*, Guilford, CT: Stackpole Books (2017)

Weidinger, Otto, *Das Reich 1943–1945*, Volume V, Winnipeg: J. J. Fedorowicz Publishing Inc. (2012)

INDEX

Figures in **bold** refer to illustrations.